A DOOR INTO ANOTHER LAND

Appalachian Trail Memoirs

Chris "Windscreen" Homan

my friend Chris   12/22/2014

ISBN: 1505225159
ISBN 13: 9781505225150

TABLE OF CONTENTS

PROLOGUE

Deciding to write about the Appalachian Trail hike is no small endeavor. It has been undeniably fun, thoroughly healthy, and a progressive journey—kind of like the trail itself (only not as rigorous).

This adventure begins, as many of mine do, with a book. I first read about the Appalachian Trail (called the AT by hikers) in Bill Bryson's *A Walk in the Woods*, which presents an entertaining tale of the author's experience on most of the trail. I had just moved to New Mexico and was finishing off the last of my thirteen years in the air force.

I became an avid Bryson reader in 2005, when my great friend Young Nate gave me *Neither Here Nor There: Travels in Europe*, for my birthday. It gripped me the whole way through. The way the author wrote about traveling, drinking with new and old friends, and the unique sights and experiences around him was an entertaining mix of British and American wit. I immediately began looking for more of his books, and within a year I had read them all. I was particularly taken by Bryson's book about the AT; I had never paid much attention to long-distance hiking before, and his book would make a permanent mark on my life.

I became enthralled by the history of the AT, which Bryson so respectfully and thoroughly describes in *A Walk in the Woods*. I wanted to see for myself all that Bryson talked about: the friendly culture that long-distance hikers share, the unparalleled beauty of nature, the undiscovered charm of small-town America, and the enlightenment of self. Of course, Bryson spends plenty of time describing the unhappy details that long-distance hikes involved (such as bad blisters, discouragement, and boredom), but I wasn't put off by any of that stuff. His tale made me think and made me laugh, but what I wasn't prepared for was that it inspired me to hike the AT myself someday. After learning how much it meant to so many hikers, and Bryson himself, I was more and more drawn to the idea of doing it.

It took me five years after I read *A Walk in the Woods* to get to a place in life where I could tackle the AT. In those years I finished my air force career and separated honorably, worked for a thankless airline for a miserable four months, and worked for two years as an acoustic systems and camera repair specialist for all of the military bases in Iraq. Those Iraq years were the most exhausting and chaotic years of my working life, but I was grateful to have the opportunity to earn a bigger paycheck than I ever had before. Not only could I finally contribute to my long-neglected retirement account, but it made my pie-in-the-sky dream of hiking the AT a sparkling reality. Troubleshooting perimeter defense systems all over a combat zone made me want to do two things: earn my master's degree in business management so I could cultivate some career options that didn't involve me being shot at, and go peacefully trekking through America's quiet splendor.

Four months after I arrived in Iraq my older brother David suffered a heart attack. He died two days after Christmas 2008. I flew back to Dallas, Texas, immediately to be at the funeral and spend time with my mom and brother Andrew, who is three years younger than me. Dad passed away after a long battle with lung cancer nine months earlier, so David's unexpected passing hit the three of us hard.

I was permitted to spend a month on emergency time off before returning to Iraq or else I would risk losing my job (the systems I was working on needed to be kept operational for defense, after all). I felt bad for leaving my mother during this difficult time, but I knew that jobs like the one I had would not last very long (and they didn't). I returned to Iraq with a heaviness to my soul and delved into my work to keep from drowning in guilt and despair. That chapter of my life was defined by personal loss, emotional pain, and the constant threat of being killed.

Iraq kept me busy. I spent a minimum of twelve hours at work every day (without weekends or holidays) and traveled maniacally all over the country to repair damaged and inoperative systems. Before I knew it, two years had passed. Toward the end of my tenure in Iraq, I applied to universities and started planning my academic future. I liked the idea of pursuing higher education in the safety of my own house in Albuquerque, New Mexico, and thanks to the GI bill, I could earn a degree without acquiring a single dime of debt.

Upon returning to the States I spent the first several weeks visiting friends and family who live in Texas (where I was born and raised) and catching up on the last two years of our lives. I celebrated Thanksgiving, Christmas, and New Year's with various groups of friends and relatives between Texas and New Mexico, all the while savoring being part of civilization again. In February 2011 I committed to Wayland Baptist University for my graduate degree. One annoying detail was that graduate courses began in the fall, which meant I had to wait until August before I could begin my classes. Without a doubt in my head, I knew that I would spend those free months hiking the AT. I needed this hike to put Iraq behind me and to heal after so much death in the family. By the time March rolled around, I had committed to my fall start date at Wayland, which meant I had to focus on AT preparation. I had read that it usually takes hikers six months to hike the entire AT, so I thought I would hike the northern two-thirds of it.

I knew nothing about long-distance hiking except from what I had read in books and online. I have always kept myself in good shape, so I hiked the Sandia Mountains near my house in Albuquerque for training. Exercising at high elevation prepared me greatly, and the more I hiked the trails, the more confident I became that I could hike for at least a day, maybe even two. I never carried more than a light pack with water and snacks, so carrying between thirty and forty pounds on my back while negotiating mountains worried me. And for four months? Ha! Who the hell was I kidding? I was fraught with doubt and uncertainty, but I persisted. The singular ambition was good for me, and I felt spiritually healthy after each hike. I wanted more.

Of all the friends I had invited, only one would hike the AT with me. Kevin, like me, had recently left the air force and had saved enough to go on an adventure for a few months. Both of us were in our early thirties to midthirties, so it wasn't a surprise to find so few people that were either willing or able to take such a large bite of insanity with me. Since neither of us had children or wives at that point in our lives, we had the rare freedom to hike long distance. Kevin is one of the best people I met in the service, and I looked forward to hiking with a great friend. We agreed to start hiking together at the end of his winter job, on Easter weekend. I wanted to get started on the AT a week before Kevin, just to see how the trail felt by myself; I was intimidated by the AT, and I wanted shakedown time.

I was getting closer to my mid-April start date, and I felt as if I was a total fraud. I read the statistics about how more than half of everyone who started hiking the AT in Georgia didn't finish in Maine. However, everyone knew my plan to hike, so I wasn't going to back out. I had told damn near everyone who would listen that I was planning to hike the AT. Then I had to explain what the AT was, since very few Texans in their thirties bothered with long-distance hikes. Besides, I was more curious than scared, and I wanted to find out where my breaking point would be. If nothing else, I would get to see the wondrous beauty of Virginia, right? When it came time to depart, I decided to make a two-day stop in Dallas to see my family one last time before I hit the AT for the next few months. My brother and his wife were supportive of my endeavor, even though they thought I was crazy for trying to do it. Mom was worried about the hike, almost to the point of asking me to not do it. She wasn't sure why I wanted to do it because I hadn't ever mentioned it and hadn't hiked much before. David's death still stung her, and my eagerness to spend my free time attempting the AT didn't please her much at all. I needed some emotional support from my family to give me a boost, especially since I felt like I was about to overwhelmingly fail. Maybe I could offer some as well.

NORTHBOUND FROM ROANOKE

A fter doing some preliminary research about Appalachian Trail hikes on the Internet, I learned that there are almost as many opinions about what the proper gear should be as there are backpacks that go on the trail each year. It became obvious to me that I would need to remain open-minded and flexible. I decided to begin hiking the trail with the gear I already had and to replace anything that didn't work. I packed all the gear I already had that the air force had issued me, as well as gear that I had already bought for the few day treks I had hiked.

Like the US Army says: improvise, adapt, overcome.

I kept a journal during the hike and have used it to convey much of the experience I had on the AT.

April 12

Last day in the house before the trip. I am fully packed, and I don't think I need to worry about having packed too heavily or too much. I'm keenly aware that if I don't finish this hike for some reason, I'll feel like a failure. The last few weeks have seen day hikes, parties, friends, and much trail preparation. I try to focus on the joy I'm feeling at this precipice of adventure.

All of the curtains are drawn, my laundry is complete, and the entire house is cleaned and tidy so that when I return in a few months (hopefully triumphant), it will be a comfortable homecoming. There is nothing left to do tonight except get my last great night's sleep in the most comfortable bed in the world.

April 15

(morning)
Yesterday I flew to Roanoke, Virginia, and today I will get onto the trail and start hiking north. I had a good breakfast at the Panera Bread next to the Best Western I stayed at last night. I got eight hours of sober sleep and woke up before my 7:00 a.m. alarm clock. On my way from Albuquerque to Roanoke, I stopped off in Texas, to spend a couple of days with the family. It was encouraging to see Andrew, but Mom was filled with doubt and concern about what must seem like a foolhardy venture. She mentioned a few times how disappointed she was that I didn't want to spend my free months nearby; I have enough stress to occupy my attention at the moment. She already made me dedicate the hike to David for her and gave me a travel bottle filled with his ashes for me to deposit on the trail. I'm sure she only means well, but this hike is about trying to put demons to rest, not give them a feeding ground. Maybe I am wrong and I need to be more sensitive to her perspective. In any case, I have lots of weeks to think about things without distractions. I am able to live a happy life without feeling bad or indebted to anyone (besides my mortgage). Iraq still lingers like a bad taste, but the diet of natural scenery should rinse it away. I got some last-minute supplies for the hike like food, bug spray, and a rain cover for my pack. I'm loaded up and ready to go. The pack is heavy as hell with food and water, but I refuse to weigh it. I am going to hike with this monstrosity on my back, and over the next several days I can figure out what I need to keep, what I need to replace, and what I can do without. See you in four months, society.

(evening)
I can't believe I'm actually hiking the AT. It was a good first day. I have seen such splendid scenery, and I am slowly getting used to the weight

of my pack. Thanks to the air force, I have a heavy and bulky sleeping bag that might have been made in the 1960s, and it takes up a lot of room in my Kelty Coyote 80 backpack (which is big enough to carry a human being). Did I pack too much? Probably. I haven't decided yet what I don't need. I'm a day into the trail, and I already have a good feeling about this hike. I got on the trail just north of Dragon's Tooth where Route 311 crosses the trail and started my journey north. I hiked to McAfee's Knob and was stunned by the view. I have never seen so many eagles in my life. There were some local hikers where the rock ledge looks over miles and miles of forests, and one of them chatted with me about what she knew about the AT. ("You're so fortunate to be able to hike this trail. You're gonna love it!") Another offered me a Bud Light, which I drank happily on the cliff with my feet dangling off the cliff. I'm sure it looked much more dangerous than it actually was. My new friends let me know that bad weather was rolling in, and I didn't want to be caught in treacherous conditions on my first night. I've never hiked in inclement weather before, and I'm eager to avoid it. Before sunset, I bade farewell to the local hikers and left the knob to find a shelter. I continued on just one more mile until I noticed a rustic cabin on the right side of the trail. No one was there, so I thought it would be a good place to settle in after my first day. I unpacked my stuff and was eager to eat some trail mix and relax with my book *Zen and the Art of Motorcycle Maintenance*.

An hour after I arrived at the shelter, two thru-hikers nicknamed Big Country and Face Jacket showed up and got settled in as well. We immediately became friends and chatted about trail conditions, where we were from, and what we were carrying. They were full of good advice, and I began learning how to behave like a thru-hiker from them. We laughed and chatted loudly over the thunder and rain that came before nightfall.

The first night I spent hiking the AT was during one of the worst storms Virginia had in years. Not only was the rain loud and obtrusive, but the lightning was dangerously close. Trees were buffeted harder than usual, and their branches fell threateningly from lethal heights. The night indoctrinated me to some of the most terrifying weather I would experience over the next few months, which made me cherish the tranquil nights.

The mix of excitement and nervousness on that fifteenth of April was unlike any I had ever felt before. Nobody pressured me to do this hike; in fact many of my friends were confused and didn't understand why I wanted to do it. This is something AT hikers have in common. No matter what inspired us to hike the AT, we were urged to traverse almost twenty-two hundred miles. I felt like I was in over my head, and I had no idea what I was in for. It was an overwhelming sensation to accept a task that would hurt me more each day until I gave up; it was made easier when I remembered that all I had to do was walk at my own pace. As every hiker says, "hike your own hike." The more I heard those words, the more I took them to heart.

April 16

The weather has been severe today as well, and the three of us decided to stay put since there were falling branches and flashes of lightning. Besides, we were just too comfy in our sleeping bags, watching the nasty weather outside the shelter blowing harshly. The shelter has done a great job of keeping us and our things dry, with mist blowing in only occasionally. Big Country and Face Jacket have told me many stories of their journey from Springer Mountain in Georgia; I'm becoming more and more excited about this hike. They are still enthusiastic, even after hiking almost seven hundred miles.

For lunch I decided to use my stove for the first time. I poured SuperFuel into the stove, lit it, and wrapped the aluminum windscreen around the stove to keep the wind from blowing out the flame. I turned away from the stove to get a packet of rice from my food bag, and when I turned my attention back to the stove, the flame had engulfed the stove! In less than four seconds, the SuperFuel had turned the small flame into a hungry inferno; the heat was actually melting the aluminum windscreen as if it were made of plastic. There was no blowing out the fire, and in a one shot, I kicked the stove setup outside to be extinguished by the wind and rain. There wasn't any damage, and I was glad I caught the fire before it got out of control.

Big Country, Face Jacket, and I all read the bottle of SuperFuel that I used to fuel the stove and noticed that instead of denatured alcohol, I had accidently gotten a container of white gas. The shelter echoed with laughter, mine included. We all learned a lesson about the difference between white gas and denatured alcohol. Face Jacket let me use his denatured alcohol to cook with, so I ate and calmed down from the incident. We stayed under the shelter until late into the evening, when the storm finally passed. By then, none of us bothered to pack up and move through the soaked woods. Instead, we made a campfire (powered by the rest of my explosive SuperFuel) and relaxed under the stars and dripping trees. A southbound hiker named Suicidal stopped in at the shelter and stayed the night. He chatted nonstop about things he didn't like about other hikers and the trail. We were all glad that Suicidal was going in the opposite direction from us; he had a negative demeanor that was grating. I hope most hikers are like Face Jacket and Big Country instead of Suicidal.

I am eager to see what this adventure has in store for me for the next four months. My new friends invited me to hike with them when we leave the shelter tomorrow, and I think that I will—as long as I can keep up with them.

When I started beating feet on the trail, I merged with hikers who had started their hike two months and seven hundred miles earlier. At this point, anyone who was hiking from Georgia was all but certain to make it to Maine, since most dropouts didn't make it as far as Roanoke. This was helpful to me: I asked for advice from these seasoned hikers and was all ears about how to lighten my load and plan logistically for food and town overnights. I took notes about certain types of gear as well. By the time they got to Catawba, Virginia, most hikers had worked up to a fifteen-miles-per-day average. They encouraged me to push myself harder and longer to keep up with them than if I had been surrounded by new hikers.

April 17

This morning I woke up at 7:30 a.m. and headed out at 8:00 a.m. I wanted to be the first out from the shelter because I knew the better hikers would catch up in no time. I actually felt kind of awful for underhiking the first day and not progressing yesterday, so today I hiked seventeen miles. I feel great, except my feet are painfully blistered. I made it to Daleville after hours of perseverance and met up with Face Jacket at the motel where was staying. The day was encouraging and educational, but I will need to make some adjustments if I am going to continue this for several more weeks and months. I thought I packed everything so efficiently, but I found, after some actual hiking, that nothing can be as efficient as knowing what I am prepared to give up and do without for weight loss and a quicker pace.

Face Jacket is a good guy. I took him up on his suggestion to split a room in Daleville so that we both only spent twenty bucks to sleep on real beds at a Howard Johnson. The Negra Modelo and Yuengling beers are sitting well with me, and the day's accomplishment gives me a first taste of progress on the AT. Face Jacket looked through my supplies and offered some suggestions that will help me pack better. Now I have an idea what I should discard or replace so I can take this hiking gig seriously. I don't think that my military-issued sleeping bag will stick around, especially when there are sleeping bags on the market that are much lighter, smaller, and warmer. I also don't think I'll need a towel or my jacket liner, which takes hours to dry. I must give it some more thought; I haven't even scratched the surface of what it means to hike such long distances. I hope I am strong enough and resilient enough for the task.

April 18

Today was a simple 5.5-mile hike out of Daleville to Fullhardt Knob Shelter. I think I will be spending the night here alone, but I like it. The sky is clear and full of stars. Where some might feel loneliness, I feel peace and simplicity. Before I left Daleville this morning, I replenished supplies and replaced just a few items that weren't of sufficient quality, took up too much space, or were just too heavy. The season feels as crisp as autumn, except that the leaves are all green. The wind is soft, and it comforts me as I relax in the new, lightweight long underwear I purchased from an outfitter in Daleville (I gave a homeless man my air-force-issued winter underwear, which was warm but bulky). Peace of mind distracts me from the punishing blisters on both heels. I feel content, in pain, and relaxed all at once. I remind myself to not be distracted too much by things that aren't here, like I did when I was stationed in the Middle East for years at a time. I need to see what is here, enjoy the present, and absorb the journey. I shouldn't be worried whether I have hiked too little or where my hiking friends are. I am hiking my own hike, and I love it. I've wanted this for a long time, and it would be pointless to let my mind stray from this hike. That is easier said than done, but it continues to be my goal. I look forward to some outdoor reading and a pleasant slumber. The last few nights I have heard deer rustling and hope to see some soon. I hear birds that sound a lot like human laughter and some that sound just like Puerto Rican tree frogs.

There are wild chives growing all along the trail here in Virginia, and they make for a delicious snack. I miss home, but I do not want to leave this place. Although I am one-third along the AT, I look forward to meeting hikers that started hiking in Springer because they will help me to make it to the finish. My bag felt more comfortable today, and I am enjoying the miles in this environment. I don't have the voracious appetite that the others have, but I'm sure that will come when I start devouring more miles every day.

Other than having the worst blisters of my life, I am content.

April 20

Good morning. I stayed at Bobblets Gap Shelter with Face Jacket and three older section hikers (one of whom sounded exactly like Albert Brooks—it was uncanny). The stream was right by the shelter, and the campfire kept the bugs away. I cooked food on my new stove properly for the first time, and the broccoli and cheese rice was yummy. I've been able to drink from streams and water sources without incident, and I use Aquamira water treatment drops to purify each bottle. The sleeping bag is heavy and bulky, but it is very comfortable at night.

After a few days of Face Jacket trying to come up with a trail name for me (SuperFuel, New Mexico, and Firestarter just didn't hit me right), he finally delivered.

"How about we call you Windscreen?"

I thought about it for a few seconds. Somehow, I doubted anyone else on the trail had used Windscreen as a trail name before, so I liked that it was unique. It would also serve as a constant reminder to me of that first night.

"Yeah, all right then."

"Seriously?"

"You bet, man—from now on, call me Windscreen!" The name would be my trail name for every hike for the rest of my life.

I have two small blisters on my left ankle and a *monster* blister on my right ankle, so I'm not sure if today will be a six-mile day or a thirteen-mile day. Yesterday was thirteen miles, and my feet could not keep up with my energy. It seems that the years of cardio have done some good; I have just never exercised with so much weight on my back before. The privy (bathroom) here is the best I have seen on the trail so far. It was built to accommodate handicapped users, which is odd since I don't expect many handicapped people make it this far away from civilization, especially down this winding ravine! Maybe I'm wrong. If they do, I feel happy knowing that they can take a shit in total comfort. Time for me to pack up and collect some water. My breakfast will be a mint chocolate Clif Bar.

(evening)

What a day. I might have made it farther along than I did if I hadn't taken a wrong turn into Buchanan, which added an extra five miles. I sucked it up and made it back to where I missed the turn that followed the AT and hiked to Bearwallow Gap; there I stocked up on more water and cooked potatoes for lunch (to which I added wild chives I picked along the trail, and they were scrumptious). The afternoon was *heavenly*. I moved like a machine; the wind was cool and kept the sweat off my body. I am enthralled to see another mountain range rolling beside me covered in vivid green trees that would make any photograph more beautiful. When I began hiking after lunch, a deer wandered closer to me than any had before. It dashed off before I could grab my camera, but I still liked being so close to it. Now I keep my camera pouch strapped to my waist belt instead of in my pack for quick access. I was energetic enough to hike farther than I did yesterday. I wanted to hike another six miles, but my blistered feet protested, so I took comfort in the ten miles I covered. I think I'm still carrying too much, both in clothes and in food, and I think I might have to reassess how much I need on this hike. I know my journal isn't light either, but I will not part with it, ever.

One of the oldest and best hikers I've met this week named Pa Bert offered me a "buckeye" that his wife made for him. It is a sumptuous ball of chocolate and creamy peanut butter, and it satisfies a craving I didn't know I had. He also suggested that I look into getting different shoes to help with the blisters. I have been hiking in heavy, sturdy hiking boots, and my feet have actually swollen since I started the hike, so I definitely need a larger shoe size. Maybe I should try hiking in trail runners instead? My feet are eager for some kind of change, so maybe I should get a pair when I get to the next town with an outfitter.

April 21

I'm sheltered tonight at Cornelius Creek after a twelve-mile hike. Tomorrow will just be a five-mile jaunt for two reasons: the next shelter after that one is twelve miles farther and my blisters are limiting the number of miles I can hike per day. The rumor is that tomorrow will be filled with rain, which dampens my spirits as well. Yesterday I gave a day hiker my heavy jacket liner, my shampoo, two pairs of socks, a couple of shirts, an extra pocketknife, and my soap. I'm also leaving behind *Zen and the Art of Motorcycle Maintenance* when I leave this shelter. I finished it, and it has been a great companion to begin the trail with. I hope that someone finds it and enjoys it as much as I did. What a great read.

It must be said that heavy shoes are not meant for long-distance trail hiking: I need trail runners. I look forward to having lighter feet; maybe wider shoes will suit me better as well. There is just no relief from these boots, no matter how much rest I give my feet throughout the day.

I met two other hikers today: one was named Sleepy and he gave me and Face Jacket some "special" fudge that made the evening swimmingly pleasant. Another hiker called Spam stopped in just for an hour to share some stories with me as he rested, but then he took off because he was pressed to meet his dad in a week and needed to make a certain number of miles each day. He seemed like a cool guy, but I doubt I'll see him again. I have a feeling I'll catch up to Face Jacket and Sleepy tomorrow, maybe even before they leave their shelter. Face Jacket never likes to leave early in the day like I do.

I hope I can get phone reception soon. I should let Kevin know where I am: ahead of schedule and almost where we agreed to meet up. Tonight completes my first week on the AT, only eighteen more.

April 24 (Easter Sunday)

I caught up with Face and Sleepy the following morning at the next shelter up the trail, where they crashed for the night. I continued on to complete my second seventeen-mile day. It rained all day, which made me happy to discover that this pack cover keeps everything inside the pack dry. Rearranging my supplies in the pack and pulling the adjustable straps tight made for *much* better control, balance, and less strain on my shoulders. My painful blisters made uphill trekking slow going, but I kept on trucking. I exchanged a few quick greetings with a few thru-hikers who passed me: Sensei, Face (not Face Jacket), the Three Bears, the Corsican, and d'Artagnan. I look forward to when I am hiking like a pro; then I might be as fast as these guys. I was cold and ready to rest my feet when I finally got to Matt's Creek Shelter. A cool section hiker called Otto had a fire already blazing, so I stayed and chatted a bit with the other section hikers who told me a few things about the small towns nearby. Sleep came early; I didn't put up a fight.

After a great night of sleep, I made oatmeal for breakfast and got going at 9:00 a.m. It was a relatively late departure, but I didn't have far to hike. In fact, it only took me forty minutes to get to the James River footbridge. I caught up with the Three Bears and d'Artagnan, who had all passed me the previous day as if I were standing still. I planned to make a side trip to Glasgow, where I had arranged to meet up with Kevin, six miles off the trail. Other hikers told me that if I collapsed my trekking poles and put them away, I would be more likely to hitch a ride. Since I had never hitchhiked before, I followed their advice.

I had been walking along the road for less than ten minutes when a pretty girl picked me up and let me ride in the back of her pickup truck. When we got to Glasgow, I hopped out and thanked her for being my first hitchhiking experience. She happily waved me good luck on my journey. The sun came out as I walked into town, and the warmth felt good all the way down into my bones. The town is tiny, but friendly. I made my way to the hiker-friendly library where I could message Kevin and see when and where we would meet up. I had full phone reception, so I called him and found out he was just thirty minutes away at his cousin's house. The news was better than I expected; I imagined we wouldn't meet up until tomorrow. I accepted the offer to hang out with them for a couple of days and be their guest at their family Easter barbecue. Kevin's luggage had been lost from his flight from Arizona, and I told him I would wait with him until he got everything and we could get back on the AT together.

It was great to see Kevin again. I hadn't seen him since he stopped through Albuquerque on his way to Arizona six months ago. It was then that I told him about my goal to hike the AT, and he surprised me by agreeing to do it with me. I'm glad he didn't change his mind.

The last couple of days have been delightful. I showered, did laundry, charged my phone and my Kindle, and enjoyed an unbelievable amount of food and good company. I called Mom and Andrew for the first time since I started the hike. Andrew and Shannon wished me good luck, and Mom reminded me to sprinkle David's ashes on the trail, which will make her happy.

Kevin's cousin Brian told me about the Yuengling Brewery up in Pennsylvania, and I am planning to go off trail to visit it. I love this adventure more and more. I am enduring the aches and blisters, but I'm rewarded with unique vistas, great people, and peace of mind. Since the airline informed him that his luggage was received in Roanoke and would be delivered to the house today, we will be hitting the AT in just a few hours.

April 26

Day two of hiking with Kevin: so far, so great. The weather is occasionally rainy, but overall it is bright with refreshing breezes. Yesterday we hiked to the Seely/Woodworth Shelter; it made for a long day that gave us fresh blisters. Today brought us past Spy Rock, which was fun to look around and see amazing 360-degree views of the area. We were both motivated to rest our feet, so we held up for the night at the Priest Shelter. I intend to sleep soundly tonight because tomorrow will be a sharp descent of Priest Mountain, which will be tough on my toe blisters. I prefer uphill climbs to descents, so tomorrow poses a challenge.

It has been great catching up with Kevin. He is fun to be around and is as optimistic as I am. It is good to have someone with me who I know and trust.

I didn't meet very many hikers in the air force, so it is rare that I can describe one culture to the other. My air force experience brought so many hardworking, thoughtful, well-meaning, and interesting people into my life. In a different, but no less important way, so did the AT. I relish it whenever I meet an individual that is the best of the armed forces who is also a long-distance hiker. Both cultures represent parts of me that I take to heart. How could I not? These are two aspects of proud, worthwhile, and demanding characteristics. I wish more of my friends could comfortably wear both hats.

April 27

Awesome day. I left with Kevin about 8:00 a.m., and we made Maupin Fields our destination. Today was ten difficult miles, tomorrow will be sixteen easier miles, and the day after will be five easy miles into Waynesboro; that makes three more days of these foot-albatrosses. Yesterday we shared the shelter with Hirsch, who chatted energetically about the evils and unnecessary nature of money. Although I thought his disdain for money was misdirected, I loved hearing about his five years of cycling around the world. Should the day come when I am ready to bicycle around the world, he will be the first person I try to get on the horn.

I was intimidated by the five-mile descent of Priest Mountain, but I was pleasantly surprised by how my toes held up. The last three miles were the most challenging to my sores and blisters, but they were also the most stunning I have ever hiked. The trail had sharp uphills and descents, several creeks to cross, and rocks made slippery by the constant rain. I liked the weather, though; it had a refreshing effect and kept me in good spirits. The terrain was difficult, but I got an excellent workout. I've decided that I will mail these heavy boots back home and get a pair of trail runners as soon as we get to Waynesboro.

I only see section hikers wear boots like these, and everyone who covers any decent amount of mileage wears much lighter footwear. During my first week on the trail, Pa Bert pointed out the simplest observation: that we lift our feet up and down and put so much weight on them independently. In my case, it amounts to around 210 pounds on each foot countless times a day. It didn't make sense to wear such heavy, slow-to-dry shoes when there were more sensible options out there. I guess my feet are smarter than I am; I'd better listen to them.

I met a thru-hiker named Squash today, and he is upbeat and easy to chat with. Like so many others on the AT, he enjoys the challenges and offers excellent conversation.

After a couple of weeks on the AT, I realized that I didn't need all the articles of clothing I was carrying, and I situated everything in my pack so that it didn't work against me. I'm not the only person who brings more than they need on the AT; everyone does. Part of the hiking experience is realizing that we don't need as much to get by as we think we do. Big Country told me that what we pack reflects our fears, and that has stuck with me since.

April 28

Today started off rainy, but the sky cleared up beautifully by lunchtime. The trail itself was strewn with broken branches and other debris left by the storm. Even the privy shelter here at the Paul C. Wolfe Shelter had been destroyed by a fallen oak branch, but fortunately it was still serviceable. This is the best shelter I have seen on the trail thus far. There is space enough for twenty sleeping bags, and more than enough hooks to hang clothes to dry (which we desperately needed after the last couple of wet days). There was a small waterfall and stream just a few steps from the large covered porch. It made for a tranquil rest after sloshing through all those miles. I bathed in the stream and rinsed out all my clothes. The plan is to crash in Waynesboro tomorrow night so we can stock up on food and other items we decided we needed (like trail runners). I will mail Mom a birthday card, too.

As I walk I am impressed by all the friendly people I have met on the trail: Spam (who met his dad so they could hike the Shenandoahs together), Squash (who just passed his bar exam and will become a New York lawyer after his hike), Hirsch (who hates capitalism but is as voracious a traveler as I am), and all of the section hikers who get to hike this trail whenever they want.

Several people had been killed by local tornadoes while we were sleeping in tents overnight that week. It was frightening to think what could have happened if the weather had been closer to the AT. With very little defense against the elements, it pays to remain alert and keep an eye on the sky. I adopted the same attitude that kept me calm in Iraq, which was to keep on going and not to worry about random out-of-control occurrences.

April 29

We left that amazing shelter and hiked two leisurely hours to the road that led to Waynesboro. It was easy to find a friendly local man to pick us up at the trail crossing and drive us into town, but not after he gave us a tour of the little town and pointed out all the landmarks that were of interest to hikers like us. We decided to get settled in at the YMCA, which allows hikers to tent on their grassy field for a tiny fee. The facility also let us have free showers, soap, smiles, warm conversation, and security for our packs.

I got some trail runners to replace the unforgiving bastards that had been punishing my feet for the last couple of weeks. It was pleasant to walk around the little town and admire the quaint homes with large, manicured lawns. Kevin and I thought that Ming's Chinese Buffet would be perfect for lunch, so we went there first and filled up three plates each and still had room for ice cream. I never tasted such good buffet food. Soon we will head to the bar, perhaps even run into Squash, and enjoy several well-earned beers. Kevin has proved time and time again since we were stationed in Okinawa what an excellent drinking buddy he is, and I'm going to drink until I get my fill.

Tonight will be the first time I actually sleep inside my tent, and I'm eager to see how it suits me. I mailed my heavy boots home and sent Mom her birthday card, which should arrive on her birthday next week. I will call her tomorrow in the morning after breakfast to wish her a happy Mother's Day so that she feels remembered on both of her special days. I'm impressed by the "trail angels" who are so eager to chat with hikers, assist with rides and food donations, and help us along our way. It is a level of camaraderie that I haven't seen since I was in the military, and I am in total awe of it. I wish I could tell everyone that helps me just how very grateful I am, and I don't know how to pay them back for it. OK, enough rambling—it's time for a few pints of Yuengling!

April 30

Last night we went to the Oasis, and I had six or seven tallboys and a couple of shots of Jägermeister. I danced with a pretty local girl, but I wasn't very coordinated. She enjoyed my company, and I hers, but we kept our clothes on. I barely remember drunk shopping at Kroger on the way back to the tent at midnight. My own bad breath woke me up at sunrise, but the tent proved to be comfortable, spacious, and easy to pack up again, even though I had a pounding skull-ache. A western omelet at Wheezy's was exactly what I needed, and it worked wonders on last night's debauchery. I called Andrew last night and had a drunken chat, and I called Mom this morning to have a hungover chat. Neither of them understands my desire to hike to Maine, but at least I have their support.

Today has been my favorite day of hiking so far. The weather is as perfect as I could imagine, and feeling the cool breeze is like drinking energy. We left Waynesboro at noon and staggered into the Shenandoahs with Squash and his friend from home called Prom Date. Today was an easy seven miles, and tomorrow will be thirteen. I will shoot for twenty-one the day after that, if my body still feels as good as it does today. I am eager to break that twenty-mile wall, and I want to do it without feeling broken and beaten. If this is what hiking in proper shoes is like, I'm going to enjoy this hike even more than I dreamed. Each step feels like I am floating, like the weight doesn't press me down as much as it should.

May 1

The thirteen miles I hiked today felt the way that five miles used to—maybe even better. No blisters, no aching back or shoulders, and my feet are still grateful for the new shoes. I feel like I should be hiking twenty miles, but I don't want to leave Kevin behind. He is content with hiking shorter distances, and he enjoys taking his time. I wake up earlier and take off before him in the mornings, and today I had a motor on me that just didn't stop. I'm finally getting my "trail legs," and they feel great.

The logbook at the Blackrock Hut Shelter shows that Face Jacket stayed here two nights ago. If he takes a "zero"—a no-hiking day—I might see him again, but he hikes such big, fast days, I doubt that I will catch up. I enjoyed hanging out with him, but I'm glad he is hiking his own hike. This shelter is hosting the Three Amigos (Leaf Guy, South Butt, and Pepper), Squash, Prom Date, Yeller, Heavy Metal, Pam, Kevin, and me. These Shenandoah shelters are big and user friendly, so it is possible for so many of us to stay here at the same time to cook, play cards, and hang out without it being too crowded. I started reading *Inside of a Dog* by Alexandra Horowitz, which is about how dogs perceive us and their environment. It is my first book to read on Kindle, and I must say I like it better than reading conventional books. I don't have to keep pages from flapping with the wind, and all I need to turn the page is to press a button, which makes for better reading in the sleeping bag. These Shenandoahs are famous for having bears, so I have been keeping an eye out for them.

I cannot overstate how blissful it is to finally develop trail legs, especially when wearing the right kind of shoes. Even now, I can remember the deep relief my feet experienced once I stopped being stubborn and changed my shoes. When I finally wore something suitable for my feet, I knew that I was going to make it to Katahdin. It took me two full weeks of hiking before I could finally feel like a real hiker; I began to actually see myself summiting that Appalachian terminus. Shrugging off the possibility of quitting was deliberate; I'll never forget how triumphant it made me feel, even though it was still early in the hike.

I should also point out how much I loved bringing my Kindle on the hike. I couldn't think of a better way to carry so much literature while taking up such little space. For a voracious reader, nothing beats having one of these e-readers to keep the mind sharp during those sunset evenings and lazy midday breaks.

The combination of relentless exercise, relaxing in the woods, and meeting a new social group was a constant source of joy. I decided that I would see the top of Katahdin. The hikers I encountered were just as determined as I was, and we stuck to each other as much as we could.

May 2

Another thirteen miles today, but today was out of the ordinary (if there is an "ordinary" out here). After the first eight miles, the group of us decided to have lunch at the wayside restaurant, since we had been anticipating, with severe hunger, to drink their renowned blackberry milkshakes. My lunch included a couple of milkshakes, a Philly cheesesteak, French fries, Sierra Mist (first time in a decade I drank soda), and a Yuengling for dessert. In fact, we all had beers to celebrate the enjoyable day. After a few relaxing hours at the picnic tables, we put on our socks and shoes and hiked the last five miles to our shelter. Hiking has been thoroughly enjoyable with the new trail runners—happy feet, indeed. Pam agreed to buy a bottle of cabernet sauvignon if I would carry it to the shelter, so I did. I'm looking forward to some good wine and good company by the campfire with more new friends.

The Amigo named Leaf Guy is easy to chat with, especially since we both enjoy talking about Nepal (where I hope to visit), college, and long-distance hiking. My pace is at the point where I can keep up with the hikers that started at Springer in March. These people are intoxicating to be around, and I want to keep their company. Some AT hikers have ridden their bikes around the world, some are ex-military like me and Kevin, some have traveled all over the world, some have been in the Peace Corps, and some are traveling outside home for the first time. This is a culture that I will enjoy being a part of, however briefly.

May 3

Kevin (aka Riverguide, thanks to Squash and Prom Date) and I hiked our first twenty-mile day. The weather was excellent with sunshine pouring through the trees, making it warm. So warm, that I took off my shirt so I could mop my brow, since I rarely stop for breaks. I was tired, but not exhausted, and I can see this pace happening more frequently. I passed the Three Amigos and made it to the shelter we all agreed to stop at. There was a small general store open near the shelter, so I took the opportunity to acquire a couple of cold dollar beers. The Amigos made it to the store shortly after, and we sat in the parking lot eating and drinking. They offered to pay for my beer since I got yesterday's, so I gratefully accepted. Kevin (Riverguide, I mean) made it three hours after I did, so I was glad that the extra-long day didn't cramp his hiking pace. Rumor has it that this shelter is frequented by bears, but tonight they must be off at some other shelter. I did see a deer, though; I could tell he wanted some of my beer, but he didn't get any. I pointed him toward the store where we got ours, and he sprinted on spindly legs toward it, never looking back.

May 5

Happy birthday, Mom! Hiking fifteen miles into Luray today. For the first time I knocked out a distance of ten miles at a three-hour pace, so I feel like a champion. Mom and I talked on the phone, and she sounded enthused about my hike. She told me that Osama bin Laden had been caught by Seal Team Six, so that became the first major piece of outside news to happen on the trail. Kevin, Squash, and I (Prom Date returned home) decided to split a Budget Inn room for the night and head out tomorrow to hike fifteen miles. I do enjoy these little town breaks; heaven knows how I savor these showers to rinse off the dirt crust from my legs, arms, and face. The beer is pretty nourishing as well. I am going to sleep warm tonight; the last couple of nights have been surprisingly chilly. I wished I had brought gloves when I took off from the shelter this morning, but after twenty minutes of brisk hiking, I was comfortable. I enjoyed hanging out with the Three Amigos and Squash this week; I hope our paths will cross again. Kevin and I drank a couple of bottles of wine last night; they were so good, I'm still savoring the taste today. Still no bears in sight; maybe they're hibernating.

May 6

Perfect hiking day. Even after having eight beers after my journal entry last night, I woke up feeling great this morning. Squash and I went to the manor house near our hotel to access its Wi-Fi with our Kindles and then returned to the inn hungry for breakfast, but found only a few small boxes of apple juice and some marshmallow and chocolate cookies. That wasn't good enough for me, so I went to Uncle Buck's across the street because it looked like a good chance for me to have a heartier breakfast, and I was right. I had rainbow trout, eggs, fried potatoes, and coffee for nine dollars. Then the three of us got a ride from a helpful local to the AT trailhead, nine miles away. Gorgeous weather shone upon us for fifteen miles, and I ran into a hiker I met several days ago, named Johannes, who joined us for blackberry milkshakes, two beers, and a forty-five-minute break at the Wayside about halfway into the hike. I am enjoying this journey; I find myself looking forward to the fifteen-mile hike we have planned for tomorrow. Tonight, I am enjoying the tent, which gives me a relatively private place to relax before bed, but I feel like I am still with the group. I almost feel as if I don't deserve the great times this trail is sharing with me.

I have fond memories of little Luray. Like an oasis in the desert, small towns like this one offer so much just by providing an Internet connection, a shower, and some kind of enclosed shelter. I loved checking out the different stores and supermarkets, seeing the various selections that differed from one area to the next. Shopping as a distance hiker wasn't the same as shopping like a resident; it became a fascination of mine to comb the aisles of each store to find the best foods that were lightweight, full of calories, economical, and would keep for days unrefrigerated. Every hiker has different tastes, and we gave each other lots of ideas, which made for exciting food adventures. I learned that I never get tired of eating rice, so I would always stock up on several bags of quick-cook rice meals that I would have for lunches and dinners as a reward for accomplishing each section. Hunger was a constant part of hiking the trail, so shopping for food had an almost pornographic appeal. I don't think I can ever walk into a typical supermarket again without being impressed by the immense selection, nor would I want to.

May 7

Today was eighteen rewarding miles; I feel like I just might be getting the hang of it. This morning, Squash made coffee with his Jetboil French press and shared some with me and our new friend Lala. It delighted me to know that Lala picked up *Zen and the Art of Motorcycle Maintenance* from where I left it and loves reading it as much as I did. Lala told me that I laughed a lot in my sleep last night, which entertained him. I couldn't remember my dream, so I wasn't able to shed any light on what might have made me laugh so much.

I made good time hiking, and we are getting close to Harpers Ferry. It is the symbolic halfway point on the AT, and where local pronunciation of Appalachian shifts from *ap-a-lah-chin* to *apple-ay-shin*. This shelter is exquisite. It has a covered porch, a cooking pavilion, and a comfy bench, and soon (according to the sign posted on the inside wall) it will have a solar shower. I'm here with Duck, Fig, their dog Game, Sassafras, Lala, and Kevin. Squash was tempted to stay with us, but he was intent on getting to the next shelter. Last night, Lala asked me if I think the trail will change me. I told him, after some thought, that I wasn't sure, but I thought that an experience like this has to change a person, even if it is just a little. As I thought some more, I realized that everywhere I travel, I am looking to make new friends, hear new stories, and figure out how to see more cultures. Maybe this means that I am constantly seeking to change myself.

From May 7 onward, Squash would remain just two or three days ahead of me on the trail. I always hoped that we would see each other again, and it continues to be my hope. He is, no doubt, upholding justice in some New York court as I write this. I wish him all the best.

May 8

Happy Mother's Day! I wasn't able to call Mom because I have no bars on my phone today; I must be pretty far from civilization.

I did eighteen miles yesterday, according to *The A.T. Guide* by David "Awol" Miller, and nineteen, according to the park signs. Tomorrow Kevin, Lala, and I are going to hike just ten miles to what is supposed to be a kick-ass AT-operated facility called the Bear's Den Hostel. I heard they offer AT hikers a large pizza and a pint of Ben & Jerry's ice cream; nothing sounds more delicious to me than that exact combination. Of course, I could stand to do some laundry and use the shower. Tonight, I'm crashing with Lala, Joe, Duck, Fig, Game, Johnny Appleseed, Mango, and Kevin; so my company is of excellent quality. We exchanged stories about Big Country, who was found out to be a section hiker and might even be homeless.

I keep thinking about the direction my life is headed. I should try to spend more of my life in vocations that provide nonmilitary travel and enough pay to get by without begging or borrowing. Also, I should spend time with open-minded people and make more time for outside activities instead of going to the gym all the time. I feel healthier than ever. I'm feeling a little bit high now—and it's awesome.

May 9

I woke up this morning with a fever, a fever whose only cure was pizza and ice cream. I attacked the ten miles of the "roller coaster," a series of constant ascents and descents all the way to the Bear's Den Hostel, in just four and a half hours. The day was absolutely gorgeous. This hostel reminds me of a European castle, which makes sense since it was built in the 1930s by a European family whose sense of architecture evokes hospitality and comfort. I called Mom on Kevin's phone because mine had no reception. It was awkward at first because she was upset that no one called her to wish her a happy Mother's Day yesterday, but only at first. The twenty minutes we spoke were only about my hiking progress and how I needed to be careful. If she knew about all the wonders the trail has presented to me in vistas, characters, and moments of spiritual awakening, she might understand why I am motivated to do something like this.

It was so nice to eat pizza and watch *Orange County* with Kevin and Lala tonight, while we combined our clothes and shared laundry duties. My clothes actually smell *great,* and I am looking forward to the fifteen miles we are planning to hike tomorrow, the first four of which will finish the dreaded roller coaster. Kevin and I both need to resupply soon, because there isn't much here in the way of food. I am learning how to pace my resupplies better to coordinate with my hiking and consumption rates and am discovering more and more about myself with each mile.

May 10

Fifteen miles. It was difficult to leave the Bear's Den Hostel today, but I pried myself away at 9:15 a.m. Once I got going, I didn't stop for ten miles until I reached the next shelter and rewarded myself with a two-hour break. I finished *Inside of a Dog* and started reading *Dracula* by Bram Stoker. I love this Kindle; it's like carting around an entire library that weighs less than a single book. What is not to love for the traveler on the go? I made it to a cozy little campsite surrounded by tall trees; not only is it a comfortable place to relax, but surprisingly I get full reception on my phone. Back in Luray I had no reception, but here in the wilderness, I have four bars. I made use of my good fortune by chatting with Andrew about Mom, my hike, his goings-on, and his birthday, which is coming up in ten days. He forgot to call Mom on Mother's Day; either that or he didn't feel like facing her negativity (which I could definitely relate to).

Man, I can't wait to replenish my food supply tomorrow; I have decided to make it a totally vegetarian affair. I am taking a cue from Mango, a thru-hiker who has shown remarkable progress for a vegetarian. I will see how the change in diet works for me. I am always looking for ways to become healthier, so maybe if I cut back on eating meat on the trail, it will make the meaty foods I eat during town visits even more special. Mango, Johnny Appleseed, and Riverguide—are camping at this site with me, so it is another night of laughter and excellent company. In a couple of weeks, Kevin will take a break from the AT to attend his Arizona friend's wedding, which might be about the same time I visit the Yuengling Brewery. It is as important out here on the trail to look forward to events as much as it is in civilized life, I have noticed. As I crossed out of Virginia into a new state for the first time, John Denver's song became the anthem for the day.

May 11

Mango, Johnny Appleseed, Kevin, and I hiked the fifteen miles to Harpers Ferry and made it to the Appalachian Trail Center just before it opened, right at 8:45 a.m. We checked e-mail, let our friends and families know we weren't injured or dead, and had drinks as we looked around the place. The ATC is a welcome place for hikers, and all the pictures of hikers from the last several decades made us take stock of what it meant to be long-distance hikers on the AT. Kevin and I caught the bus to Charlestown's Walmart to restock our food bags, and true to what I told Mango, I went totally vegetarian. No pepperoni slices, no tuna, no meat products at all. I think I might have gotten enough food for ten days. When we returned to the ATC, I ran into my old friend Face Jacket. He didn't recognize me at first; I guess I look fairly different now compared to my first few days on the trail. It had been weeks, pounds, and a beard's growth since I last saw him, and we enjoyed catching up about the last several weeks. He was making plans to backtrack to Damascus, Virginia, to attend Trail Days, the AT reunion and festival. I wasn't sure if we would cross paths again anytime soon. I told him that I hoped to see him again, and I thanked him for christening me Windscreen; it fits me like a glove.

It was an enjoyable afternoon in cozy Harpers Ferry. Kevin and I looked at the outfitter and stopped in at the pub across the street. We enjoyed a few pints of local draft beer, and we chatted about what our lives might be like after the hike. He is giving some thought to river guiding until Thanksgiving and then may teach English in Thailand for a while. Bastard stole my idea! Our conversation got me thinking about what I'll end up doing after I get my master's degree, which I will begin working on after this hike. I want to do something similarly exciting and exotic, as long as I can afford my mortgage payments. I certainly have enough time to plan it out.

Harpers Ferry was a momentous part of the journey. Even though it wasn't a halfway point for us, Kevin and I still liked the character of the town. Many hikers choose to stay overnight there, but for us, a pleasant day was enough. Looking back, the entire day was perfect: the hike from the campsite to town and the hike out of town to the shelter we stayed at with Lala. The evening hike was slightly inebriated, which can be fun as long as I don't drink too much. Harpers Ferry also represents the part of the hike where I stopped being concerned with making it to Katahdin and started looking beyond. I had the entire year after the hike allotted to studying for my degree, but until Harpers Ferry, I hadn't given much thought to what kind of job I would aspire to. I knew that I wanted to eventually segue into teaching English; I love language and that is a perfect job for a traveler like me. The only drawback is that it is difficult to find a teaching job that pays a lot, so I had to consider my options and decide what my priorities were. If it was possible to make decent money, have a fulfilling job, and see the world, then it is up to me to figure out how.

May 12

Such a relaxing day. We ended up doing eighteen miles, and I took a four-hour break at the halfway point. I read a bit of *Dracula* and took a nap in the sun. Five miles before the last campsite of the day, we ran into the Three Amigos. It was a happy reunion, and we found a rocky outcropping to spread out on and get comfortable in the bright sunshine. We cooked dinner; exchanged stories about Squash, Lala, Mango, Johnny Appleseed, and others; and went to bed in our sleeping bags under the stars. It is good to be out of the Virginias, and the march of progress is undeniable as we traverse the nation bit by bit. The trees look a little bit different, and the Potomac was fun to hike alongside as we crossed into Maryland buzzed, thanks to several Harpers Ferry beers. I must admit, I have wanted to see these states for many years; I am eager to see what the rest of the hike might present.

May 13

Today began insanely early and abruptly. Kevin woke me up (first time *that* ever happened) as I felt heavy, fat raindrops slap my face. We immediately made the decision to pack up and get moving to the next trail shelter, since there wasn't any shelter from the incoming storm. We departed at 3:00 a.m. with a farewell to the Three Amigos (who crowded in the same tent made for two) and hiked for three hours through the wet, dark, foggy jungle. We made it to the shelter just after daybreak and unceremoniously hung up our wet things and bundled into our sleeping bags to return to sleep. After a four-hour nap, we headed out to hike the next fifteen miles—slow going through slippery terrain. I'm tending the fire we built and watching the dusk fall around us. It took a lot of care to watch our steps and not slip on our asses, but we made it. I'd like to night-hike again, but I'd prefer it to be dry and with a full moon. We crossed into Pennsylvania five miles ago; Maryland, as quick as it was, is now behind us. We are making good distance for a couple of newbies, but Kevin's feet are wearing him out. His complaints remind me of my first several days on the trail, so I tell him what worked for me. We heard about the half-gallon ice-cream challenge in Pine Grove, which is where we should be in about three days; we are getting mentally prepared for eating more ice cream in a single sitting than we ever attempted before. It has been one wet, cold, and long day for us; I plan to sleep like a coma patient.

That day stands out in my mind as the worst day of hiking I ever had. My glasses were foggy, it was a moonless night, the rain made the rocks treacherous to negotiate, and I wanted nothing more than to crawl into a warm sleeping bag and ignore the world. As difficult as it was, I am very glad to have hiked that morning because from that day on I knew that I could hack it, no matter the obstacles. I have hiked through rain and thunderstorms many times since then, but as long as my glasses are clear, or I have daylight, or I have gotten enough sleep the night before, I know things aren't that bad.

May 14

Good, well-paced day. Kevin wanted to keep to a sixteen-mile day, so I agreed. He will take a week off the trail soon to go to a Phoenix friend's wedding. I think when he is off trail, I will press on with more miles per day; I want to see what I am capable of. I enjoyed the morning from 7:00 a.m. until 9:00 a.m., when rain began to pour down. I already had my pack cover on, and I didn't feel like stopping to put on my raincoat, so I pushed ahead and got drenched. I hiked 10.2 miles in four hours and took my first meal of the day at the Rocky Mountain Shelter. It stopped raining at 11:00 a.m., and I hiked the remaining 5.6 miles to the Quarry Gap Shelter. This is easily the best shelter I have stayed at since the Paul C. Wolfe Shelter just before Waynesboro, Virginia. This campsite has two side-by-side shelters with a covered porch and picnic table, not a scrap of litter, and a bubbling brook, just in front of the campsite. There are even hanging plants that are well kept, making the place feel loved and cared for. It feels luxurious to spend the night here.

I had to disappoint a local hiker who asked me if I was carrying a Bible to spend time with God. I told her that I wasn't. I spared telling her that I was reading *Dracula*. Neither of us was rude, but her question was an odd one to ask as she and her company left the area. I could tell that she wanted me to read the Bible under God's great supervision, but reading the Bible once is enough for me.

Tomorrow should be another rainy day, and I actually don't mind. I am still reminded how comfortable it is to hike in daylight, so I don't might if it is rainy as long as I can see my surroundings.

May 15

Today marks my first month on the AT. I made good time today by hiking 17.5 miles in under five and a half hours. I took a break at the shelter Kevin and I agreed to stay overnight at, but made the command decision to do more miles. I thought it would feel awful to hike nineteen miles after eating a half gallon of ice cream, so I wanted to get the hiking out of the way today, instead. I am extremely glad I made that call, because now that I have all that ice cream inside me, I feel unhealthy, lethargic, and overstuffed with sickly sweetness. I went with Hershey's Neapolitan ice cream for the half-gallon challenge, and I finished the whole amount in forty-seven minutes. No record breaker, but it was a hell of an experience; one I doubt I'll ever agree to again. I'm shivering cold, and the rainy breeze is chilling me to the bone as I sit on the general store porch waiting for my friends to arrive. I can't even think of eating ice cream again anytime soon. It is drizzling now, and the rest of the week promises more of the same; I'd better suck it up and deal with it. I'm certain I will see the sun again someday!

When Kevin arrived, he ate his fill of ice cream as well. We both decided it was a bad idea that was worth doing once. There is a mansion-hostel next to the general store, which is the site of the gluttonous half-gallon challenge, but I think we will stealth camp on this store's porch. The decision has less to do with saving money, as it does with making a point. I'm not sure what that point is, but we are definitely making it to insignificant effect. The porch is wide and dry enough for the five of us, and no one is around to tell us to stop being homeless vagrants. It has been an unforgettable ice cream day with Kevin, Hermes, Pike, and Moose.

May 16

It was a beautiful night for the five of us to cowboy camp. No one bothered us; we kept out of sight and to ourselves.

The weather was good for the first half of the day until the sky opened up in a deluge. After hiking eleven miles, I took an hour-long break in an unmarked field because I started feeling woozy. I ate some Nutella and peanut butter, which made me feel better for a bit, but then the dizziness returned just a couple of miles away from our destination. My bones ached throughout my body, my joints complained, and I became more exhausted than I had any right to after an easy day like today. I felt more fatigued than at any other point since I started this hike. Eating some cheddar and broccoli rice made me feel better; I wonder if I had been suffering from salt deficiency. My guess is replacing normal food with ice cream was a worse idea than I expected, so I promised myself that once was enough for ice-cream silliness. Riverguide and I squeezed into the shelter with five other hikers and one dog. One of them shared a nip of his Maker's Mark bourbon before falling asleep, so that was welcome help. I am overjoyed to be relaxed for the night; I know sleep will come effortlessly. We are planning to hike nineteen miles tomorrow, so I hope I wake up fully recovered.

I want to get online soon and arrange a backpack swap with REI. I have heard amazing things about their customer service, and I am eager to get a smaller pack that fits me better than this behemoth; it has too much empty space, and I no longer need it.

Of course I ate ice cream after that infernal challenge, but I'll never forget the horrible existence that I endured for the whole day after cramming a half gallon of Neapolitan into my belly. I was reminded that day how important it is not to eat buckets of ice cream at a time, which is something I never considered learning before. Please, if you ever see me sit down with the intention to eat more than a pint of ice cream, do me a favor and stab my eating hand (my right hand) with the nearest sharp instrument. I will eventually thank you for it.

May 17

I'm back, baby! There are few things in life better than getting your normal self back after a noticeable decline, and I'm glad it was temporary.

Maker's Mark may have been responsible for my amazing recovery. Note to self: eat less ice cream, drink more Maker's Mark.

I must confess that I am looking forward to tomorrow's eleven-mile hike into Duncannon. Rumor has it the hotel there is cheap and hiker friendly: no two adjectives are more welcome to my ears. Laundry and showers are past overdue, and a dry change of clothes are worth real money at this point. It has been constantly rainy or overcast the last several days, with only brief glimpses of sunshine. I think that everyone on this part of the trail is dealing with perpetual dampness and wetness, and the sullen moods reflect that. The mist and humidity make it difficult to see through my glasses, but I'm dealing with it. I'm happy to keep a pace of 2.5 miles per hour on average terrain, and my body performance remains tip-top. It is a comfortable realization to perform consistently better than I dared to expect.

May 19

(morning)
It was a wet, but good eleven-mile hike to get to Duncannon yesterday. I didn't get to sleep until late the night before thanks to Croft's super-loud snoring, but that didn't stop my feet from working. I got into town about noon and went straight up to the Doyle Hotel. The staff and patrons made me feel welcome. I had a few pints of Yuengling after I changed into dry clothes and met some other hikers named Rambling Shamrock and Ad Cane, Bear Jew, Rock Puncher, Stormsong, and Treebeard. We chatted about where we were from and how our hikes were treating us. I told them about my plan to visit the Yuengling Brewery, and they agreed it sounded like a worthwhile venture. Rodney, an old air force buddy I hadn't seen in over a decade, heard I was hiking through Pennsylvania near his home; he offered to pick me up and hang out for a couple of days. I gratefully accepted his offer, and we agreed to meet the afternoon after I toured the Yuengling Brewery near Port Clinton.

The plan is to hike eleven or twelve more miles to the next shelter today, so we will leave town at lunchtime. Kevin is going to hike a little farther and then take off to make his flight west for his friend's wedding. I'm excited about receiving the new equipment I ordered last night. I coordinated with REI to have them send me a new smaller pack in exchange for the two-year-old pack I originally purchased from them. I also ordered a smaller, lighter sleeping bag that is rated for 20 degrees Fahrenheit, so that will take up much less room than my heavy and bulky military-issued one. Everything will be delivered to Port Clinton, where I will meet up with Rodney. I am excited to see what the new pack will feel like since it will be much smaller and five pounds lighter—not to mention seeing my old friend again.

(evening)
It was a rare pleasure to be dry for twenty hours. Moments after Kevin and I left the city limits, a thunderstorm rolled over the top of us and drenched us thoroughly. Despite the weather, it was a pretty easy eleven miles. I think I have enough food to last until Port Clinton, but I'll have to keep a careful eye on everything. Rodney hit me up on Facebook today and told me his family was looking forward to meeting me, which helped me to ignore the continuous downpour.

Before I left Duncannon, I had the most delicious veggie omelet of my life, and then I called Mom to see how she was doing. Apparently she was preparing to fill out a missing person's report since I hadn't called in ten days. Then she suggested several things that I have been thinking about all day, like how I am not responsible to anyone but myself, how it hurt her feelings that I decided to go on this hike instead of spending my free time with the family, how she thinks that I don't deal with reality and how I'm not a contributing member of our family. I don't agree with any of that, and thankfully neither does Andrew. Kevin heard me talking on the phone, so he invited me to vent about it a little bit. He assured me that she is just jealous about what I am doing. It is good to have both a brother and a friend to confide in during these occasional moments of confusion and self-doubt.

Duncannon, and the Doyle Hotel in particular, is a unique feature of the AT. I would compare it to a favorite T-shirt that your girlfriend wants you to get rid of, but you just can't bring yourself to part with. The hotel itself is run down and operates on a shoestring budget, but it is filled with the kind of heart and personality that all long-distance hikers love. Although I showered underneath a ceiling with exposed wires and we slept in beds that creaked more than a haunted house, I wouldn't have missed it for the world. Like Samuel L. *Jackson said in* Pulp Fiction*: "Personality goes a long way."*

From the moment I mentioned to Mom that I was planning to hike the AT, she was reluctant about it. I suppose it was drastically different from anything I had ever attempted before, and she was understandably surprised by my reasons and abilities. It wasn't until weeks later that she started being positive and encouraging, but occasionally she would still be offended that when I finally had some free time, I wanted to spend it hiking instead of being with my loved ones. I think this is a burden all travelers have when their loved ones don't realize how important it is to travel places and see the world. It has been a delicate but steady source of strain in my family, but the good outweighs the bad. My friends and loved ones want desperately to see more of me, which I'm willing to accommodate but not if it means giving up a life that I love.

Once again, I am stunned by the kind of folks I meet on the AT. Rambling Shamrock (Ram Sham) and Ad Cane were a pair of hikers who had more to overcome than any hiker I had ever met. Ram Sham was completely deaf; she was encouraged to hike with her friend who went by Ad Cane on the trail. Ad Cane was also deaf, but he was also almost completely blind. It had been his lifelong ambition to complete the AT, and he was eager to complete it while he still had some vision to go by. This pair was an inspiration to all who met them, and they reminded us of the strength of the human spirit against intimidating odds.

May 20

Happy birthday, Andrew! I'm celebrating his birthday by relaxing on my sleeping bag and Z Lite mattress, listening to some music, while absorbing the day. Today was special for two reasons: my younger brother's birthday and the sprinkling of my older brother's ashes. I hiked thirteen miles first thing today, and then I took a trail-mix break. I was sitting under the branches of a huge tree and noticed how particularly gorgeous this wooded glen between two streams was. I found a spot of grassy earth that was spotlighted by a ray of sunlight, as if by Providence. With all the rain lately, it was especially attractive; the colors popped vividly and the glen was simply majestic. I wouldn't describe myself as religious, but when something appeals to me spiritually I don't treat it lightly. I deposited my handful of David's ashes on that part of the AT where the flowers were wildly reaching toward the warm sunlight. I didn't cry or say anything, and there wasn't a soul around to disturb the moment; the moment felt right. His ashes looked small to me, and surprisingly insignificant; especially since they were once the skin and bones of my beloved brother. That small mound of ash that I sprinkled on the grass was not David. It occurred to me that David was who remained in my mind and my heart, not what fell to earth in granules upon the glen. He passed from the corporeal to the intangible. I thought today that although I deposited his remnants at that spot of earth, I will continue to carry David with me all the steps of my life. I'll never forget how he contributed to my world—this world.

I've given a lot of thought to what Mom told me at the Doyle Hotel. She isn't happy with my outlook on life, and I should point that out to her. She asked me yesterday if I dreaded phoning her; I lied and said that I didn't. I wonder if that was the right thing to do.

One of my earliest memories of my older brother was how he loved watching the TV show The Life and Times of Grrizzly Adams. *The show's theme song had always been one of our favorite songs, and it continues to be one of mine. When I was very young, I began to asociate distant mountaintops and the rugged wilderness with the music of David's beloved show, and spending days and days on the AT made me think of David more than ever. He would have wanted to hear everything about this adventure, and I am sad that I can never tell him. At least we both shared an appreciation of that show and that music when he was alive, and I remembered that every day on the trail. No doubt we would have talked endlessly about this journey in another land.*

May 21

Last night I was a little worried about how little food I had (just three bags of trail mix), and still three hiking days away from Port Clinton where I plan to resupply, get my new gear, and catch up with Rodney. I am looking forward to this upcoming town visit almost more than

I can bear, if only because my journey there will be a hungry one. I spoke briefly with Andrew, who was hung over from birthday celebrating yesterday. I left the decrepit Rausch Gap Shelter, and I hiked a few miles with some older, but sprightly women who were burdened with too many snacks and were eager to share them with me. I love trail magic—those unexpected gifts on the trail that inspire awe and gratitude. They wanted to hear about my hike, so I talked about the miles I hiked and the people I ran into. They reminded me how fortunate I was to be able to make the hike. They offered me energy bars, organic fruit bars, string cheese, and cashews. I returned the favor by giving them a Ziploc bag of my homemade trail mix, and they loved it. The trade was overwhelmingly in my favor, but both sides felt like they got the better deal.

I hiked seventeen miles to the bloody excellent 501 Shelter. When I arrived, I was delighted to see a couple of section hikers stoking a fire and preparing food. They shared their brats, potatoes, and hot dogs while I contributed a broccoli and spinach pizza topped with feta cheese, which I had delivered to the trailhead in just a half hour. It was a feast for the gods. Treebeard and Stormsong are sleeping in this shelter as well; we enjoy each other's company and laugh often. They spent last night at a hotel near the AT to dry off and warm up; I don't blame them one bit. The daily act of sliding soaking wet socks on over my feet before I tackle the muddy and slippery trail makes it difficult not to fantasize about sunshine and the indoors, but I am determined to make it to my next destination without complaint or delay. I hunger for Port Clinton, civilization, and a reunion with my friend from a past life. I am giddy beyond belief.

May 23

Yesterday was such an accomplished day. I didn't want to leave the awesome 501 Shelter, but I stepped away from it at 7:30 a.m., eager to make headway. Treebeard and Stormsong persuaded me to hike the full twenty-four miles into Port Clinton, and I'm glad they did. At the end of the hike I was tired, but I actually felt like I could have gone on hiking some more. What a nice little town Port Clinton turned out to be. The sharp descent to it was rewarded by manicured lawns and picturesque neighborhoods. It is green everywhere, and the constant drizzle only saturates the environment with even more color. Treebeard and Stormsong arrived in town before me since their pace is faster, especially over the rocky terrain. I made my way to the pavilion that is famous among hikers for offering free shelter; I was amazed to see that it could shelter at least fifty people, and it was furnished with tables and chairs. There were a few hiker boxes filled with assorted items like shampoo, deodorant, and shoelaces, but I admit that what I loved the most about it was that it offered cover from the rain. I was the first hiker to arrive at the pavilion, so when I changed to dry clothes and rehydrated myself, I went looking around for the nearest bar, knowing that would be the best place to find them. I was right. They had eaten well and were drinking a beer each. We all took six-packs to the pavilion to drink and discuss life, the trail, and politics until sleep took us. I didn't read my Kindle at all last night, and I fell asleep in the lounge chair wrapped in my military-issued sleeping bag one last time. Today I woke up early and excited for a day of errands: I need to find a place to screw the earpiece back onto my glasses, pick up mail, visit the Yuengling Brewery, and rendezvous with Rodney.

May 24

(morning)

Yesterday was absolutely perfect. Treebeard, Stormsong, and I had breakfast at a restaurant near the pavilion, and I had a yummy veggie omelet and coffee. From there, I was given a lift to Pottsville by a friendly old man who even showed me to a great little optical shop to get my glasses fixed. Talk about serendipity. After a week of trying to wear glasses with a lens that refused to stay in the frame, it was euphoric to be able to see again. From there, I walked to the Yuengling Brewery, stopping once on the way to eat a slice of tomato pizza and a slice of broccoli pizza at Roma's Pizza, and I washed them down with a couple of Yuenglings to prepare for the brewery. At 1:30 p.m. I joined a large group of beer-loving strangers. None of them were hikers, but we got along well. We took in the sights and learned about one of the country's best-loved beer companies. After two complimentary beers, I left to meet Rodney at a nearby Dunkin' Donuts he suggested. When he walked in, I was astonished that he looked exactly the same as he did thirteen years ago. We went to a post office in Port Clinton to pick up my shipment from REI, and then we went to Allentown, where I met his wife and children. I didn't mind having pizza for dinner; it was delicious and I was hungry. I transferred everything from the old bag into the new, and my equipment was a perfect fit. I offered Rodney my old sleeping bag, which he gratefully accepted. That night I enjoyed relaxing clean on their comfy couch and discussed how the hike was going and what we had both been up to for the last decade. I got along with his family effortlessly and was thrilled that I had the chance to meet them. Today I will tour Allentown while everyone is at work, chat with Mom, mail my old backpack to REI as arranged, and get some food for the trail.

(evening)
Laundry is clean and dry, and I sent the pack to REI for a full refund, resupplied my food, and ambled around quaint Coopersburg. These small Pennsylvania towns are like pockets from a dream; they are so delicate, serene, and impossibly lovable. The houses that line the street have grand character that I so rarely see in bigger cities; they make me feel fortunate, even just briefly, that I get to experience small-town America. There are storms predicted for the night, so I gave in to Rodney's tempting offer to stay another night and get back to the trail in the morning. It is soothing to sit with others, watch television again, and not be buffeted by the elements.

I packed my equipment in the new GoLite backpack, and I'm encouraged by the lighter load. I looked forward to hitting the trail and seeing how the new backpack and sleeping bag fare on the AT. These last two days have been remarkable. I don't know that I have ever, in just a few days, seen so much new countryside, reunited with old friends, sauntered around such cozy towns, and replenished my belly and my food bag. The morning would begin early, so I thanked Rodney and his wife for taking me into their home so warmly. I told them that should they ever venture to Albuquerque, I would gladly have them stay at my place and show them around the Duke City, but I have a feeling they won't make it out there anytime soon. You never know.

My mind keeps returning to the AT, thinking about where my trail friends were camping out tonight, would I see them again, and how many miles I would be ready to hike tomorrow. I am getting antsy and feeling just a little disconcerted about being indoors for two nights in a row when there was so much trail left to hike, but I still slept soundly.

Port Clinton, Allentown, and Coopersburg were incredible to visit. I was glad that Rodney reached out to me and invited me to his home; it was the seamless culmination of traveling and friendship that I never get enough of. I'll never forget how he looked at me after we ate dinner and asked, "So, what the hell made you decide to hike the Appalachian Trail?" We both laughed, because when we last saw each other we were both overworked, broke, low-ranking airmen stationed in northwest Florida. A lot can change in a decade, and it was good to see him content and settled into a happy life; I think he was glad to see me pursuing my dreams as well.

May 25

Today started early. Rodney woke me up at 4:30 a.m., and we left his place thirty minutes later. I stepped out onto the AT at 6:00 a.m. and began a sun-filled day of hiking. I'm glad it was dry because today was the rockiest patch on the trail I've come across. The Bake Oven Knob was impressively scenic, and the Knife Edge was exactly how it sounds: precariously balanced hiking along the edge of jutted rocks that fell sharply on both sides. I hiked about fifteen miles, and when I made it to the shelter, I just wasn't too concerned with hiking another seventeen miles to complete the thirty-two-mile day I had considered earlier. I hiked into Palmerton to enjoy the free hostel that I heard about from some day hikers and drank some Yuenglings at the bar across the street. I will sleep soundly tonight. No Falls is at the hostel as well, who is a flip-flopper from North Carolina. He hikes small distances (about five to seven miles at most each day), so I doubt I will see him after tomorrow, but he seems cool just the same. It is 9:30 p.m., and I'm absolutely beat. I wonder if I will hike seventeen miles or thirty miles tomorrow; I guess it all depends on how I feel and what the terrain is like. One thing I do know is that the new pack works wonderfully, and the sleeping bag feels great. Speaking of, it's time for zzzzzz.

I had learned to food-shop economically and pack my equipment efficiently, so I made much better use of space. With strong legs and fierce determination (not to mention a better sleeping bag and a lighter pack that would be waiting for me in Pennsylvania), I became a hiking machine. It was great to get back under the trees and sky. The sunshine fueled me as well, giving me lots of energy and motivation. I remember thinking that day how it had been a long time since I could see so far across the distance. I loved inhaling deeply from the top of Bake Oven Knob as I surveyed the Lehigh Valley beneath me.

May 26

Good seventeen miles today. It was extremely rocky, especially the ascent out of Palmerton. The Spanish omelet I had for breakfast was a great source of energy, as I moved with a quickness not often matched. I left No Falls in Palmerton as we wished each other well, and this afternoon I caught up to Patches and Backflip: a couple of cool thru-hikers I've chatted with before. I am resting by myself at the Leroy Smith Shelter tonight; it is small, but well kept. Tomorrow I plan to hike twenty miles into Delaware Water Gap and stay at the church-sponsored hiker hostel there. I'm cooking my cheese and broccoli rice for tonight, and making oatmeal tonight for tomorrow morning so I can have a quick morning with an early departure. I dislike having much to do other than pack up and go in the mornings, so I am using my evening hours to prepare as much as I can. I have just two more nights in Pennsylvania; I can't believe the time has passed this quickly. I hiked with my tunes playing today, and although it made for an extremely rhythmic day, it drained my phone battery. I found ten or twelve ticks on me throughout the day, but I brushed them off before they took hold. Periodic self-inspection makes me feel safe as I hike through these tick-ridden fields. Great breezes and warm sunshine made for a thoroughly happy day, and I dare to hope for more of the same.

May 27

Thunderstorm last night. I fell asleep at 8:20 p.m. and woke up at 9:00 p.m. to bright-as-daylight lightning followed by rain. It was loud, but I fell asleep anyway. I had the shelter all to myself, so I was able to pull all my stuff inside it with plenty of room so none of it got the slightest bit wet. I started hiking the first thirteen miles of the day at 6:30 a.m. and took a thirty-minute break at a shelter where I met Amazon, a section hiker. Amazon is a lighthearted and eager hiker, so I was glad he decided to head to DWG (Delaware Water Gap) with me. We hiked the remaining seven miles into town, and it was extremely pleasant. The weather was ideal, and it was a gentle downhill all the way those last few miles. I made my way to the hiker hostel and found a few other like-minded souls who wanted shelter, rest, and food as much as I did. After my shower, I got changed into my clean clothes and went looking for a place to fill my growling belly. I met up with Amazon as well as some new friends named Yikes and Thru at the best-looking restaurant in town; I ordered a spinach and salmon club sandwich with a bowl of New York clam chowder. That, along with a few pints of Yuengling, replenished the calories I expended today. After supper, we all agreed to look around town for dessert. We found what I thought was the perfect place: a farmers' market that offered freshly made pies of all fillings and sizes. My pie was a heavenly fruits of the forest with no ice cream or whipped cream; it was exactly what

I wanted on its own. I can tell it will be difficult to leave this place in the morning, but I am energetic and eager to hike twenty-five miles to the next shelter.

May 28

Last night was surprisingly rewarding. I was prepared for an early night, but Thru and I went to the hotel bar next door and enjoyed listening to live jazz instead. I could look out across the street and see the AT just a few steps away and thought about all the ways this trail has shown me unexpected beauty, fun people, and charismatic small-town America. After seven Yuenglings, I slept on the big couch in the common room (away from the resonating snoring) and dreamed pleasant dreams. I had a broccoli and cheese omelet (I seem to not be able to get enough broccoli and cheese on this trek) and mailed a postcard to Mom and then left DWG at 8:30 a.m. to hike the twenty-five miles I planned on. I'm here at the shelter with Pilot, Yikes, Thru, and a gazillion mosquitoes, which were distanced from our shelter by the campfire so we could relax undisturbed. The Deet does nothing, except get in my eyes when I sweat. I could see the water source here, so I didn't filter any of it. In a few days I'll know if this is a good idea or a stupid one. I don't think I should be as scared of giardia as I have been, so I'll roll the dice a little to see what happens. I loved seeing the Delaware River, and the national park that surrounds it was impressively stunning. I'm pretty fucking beat; since I ate dinner, I have had a tough time keeping my eyelids up. It's only 8:30 p.m.!

Many people have asked me what my favorite part of the AT was. Although I have no clue what that answer is, or if there can even be one, I am reminded of the Delaware Water Gap. That hike was so much fun: the weather was sublime, my new gear rewarded me all day and every day, and I met Yikes, one of my favorite people on (and off) the trail. How little I knew when I met her that we would become such great friends. Everything about DWG was friendly, comfortable, and picturesque. The food was particularly delicious, and I loved walking around and admiring the flowers and ancient, knobby trees that populated the area. The hiker hostel that we stayed at overnight was operated by a local church, and it was much appreciated by all of us. If that hostel wasn't there, I doubt I would have stayed the night in DWG and took the time to see its splendor. The AT is a smorgasbord of all kinds of rewards, and Delaware Water Gap encapsulated perfectly, for me, all that was wonderful about the hike.

May 29

The mosquitoes were ferocious last night. I had to cover my face with the sleeping bag just to ensure I had a face to wake up with. I was up at 6:30 a.m. and decided to hike another twenty-five miles today. Now that I did, I am beat again, but happy. It doesn't feel like I am actually fifty miles away from Delaware Water Gap; it feels as if I was just there a few hours ago. The ticks are plentiful but haven't posed any threats, thanks to constant body checks. I'm camping out with a familiar hiker called Pilot and a few new hikers called Herb, Spice, and Protein Powder. The day went from scrambling over rocks to easy ambling through farm fields, over streams, and on footbridges. Since I finished *Dracula* at Rodney's house, I have been reading *Idiot America*, which is an interesting, if a bit cynical commentary on the American personality. It is a short book, which I don't mind a bit. It is my second night in New Jersey, and tomorrow should be my last. I have a feeling this state will forever remind me of mosquitoes and ticks, but it will also remind me of hiking with Yikes, Pilot, and Thru. Chatting with them about our very different hiking experiences makes for interesting evenings. Today I thought about whether or not I should rent out my guest room when I get back home and start college. I will feel alone after being constantly surrounded by fascinating people here on the AT. I have time to decide. I think I will turn on my music tomorrow when I hike. Those are my favorite days.

Pilot and I reminisced about our military experiences whenever we hiked together, and we talked about being stationed all around the globe. It made me chuckle to think how the both of us saw value in this hike; or maybe I shouldn't be surprised at all. It is rare that I met any retired military

*individuals on the trail, but I liked the ones I did meet. We never stopped be-
ing fascinated by the natural beauty and remarkable people we encountered;
they were far from the kinds of people we met in the service. He agreed with
me that the military guides us along a singular perspective, whereas the
hikers who hiked the trail with us shared all kinds of different perspectives
with us in person and taught us to be more spontaneous and less concrete
with our lives. We befriended young, wealthy university students, chefs, law-
yers, preachers, musicians, writers, Walmart employees, trail runners, and
adventurers. Every soul I met was a story that never failed to entertain and
intrigue me.*

May 30

Good day today. It was thunderstorming when I woke up at 5:30 a.m.,
but by the time I ate breakfast and packed everything up, the rain
had finished for the day. I decided to hike eighteen miles, so I took it
easy this morning; I even took a two-hour break just five miles along
the trail. There was a plant market that sold local food and juices,
coffee, milkshakes, and pastries—not to mention the familiar faces
I saw there. Treebeard and Stormsong were there, as well as Niners,
Pants, Katmandu (his preferred spelling), and Stillwater. This group
of six called itself the Fellowship, and so did everyone who met them.
I spent some time at the market and enjoyed the sunshine and rest.
I liked hanging out with the Fellowship, but after a couple of hours,
I felt compelled to hike, so I got moving and arrived at the shelter at
7:00 p.m. I was happily surprised to run into Backflip and Patches. I
asked them if they minded me hiking with them into New York, and
they welcomed me, turning their duo into our triumvirate. They are
recent high school graduates, so I am encouraged that I can keep
up with hikers that are seventeen years my junior. I can tell that they
come from a more privileged segment of society than I do, but they
aren't assholes; I like them. My feet were constantly soggy today; I
thought my feet would begin to mildew. I was relieved to peel my
socks off and walk around barefoot once I got to the shelter. After a
couple of hours, they were normal again (well, as normal as feet can

look after months of punishment); I guess they just needed to dry out a bit. This morning the trail was muddy and slippery, but it got better by this evening. At 90 degrees, today has been the hottest day on the trail so far, but I am still glad to see sunshine instead of rain, so I don't mind the heat.

June 1

The three of us hiked twenty miles today. It was pretty hot, but far from unbearable. In the afternoon we happened upon a waterfall where we rinsed our heads and our bandannas. We took an hour break and spent that time exchanging stories. These are good guys, who have become interesting friends. They plan to take some time off in New York to see their family and friends, but until we split up, it promises to be a great hike together. I must admit, I was flattered earlier today when they guessed I was only twenty-seven years old. How vain I am. We were in high spirits as we crossed into New York, and I couldn't help but sing Frank Sinatra's "Start Spreading the News" at the top of my lungs. The terrain has been more forgiving the last several miles, which allows me to look around and enjoy the scenery without having to stop. I can't tell if it is because of the sunshine or the landscape itself, but these days have been so much fun. For some reason, we all felt a little lethargic late in the afternoon, but after we ate, we felt better and pressed on hiking the last of our fourteen-mile day. I came across a mailbox and sent Mom another postcard, so that made me feel like a good son. Since tonight's shelter is actually made of stone and is far away from any water sources, there isn't a mosquito or fly in sight. The three of us enjoyed watching the sunset from a rocky outcropping and reflected on how lucky we all were to find the time to make this hike. We spent the rest of the night talking about our goals after the hike and where we might be a year from now; all of us promised to stay in touch after we go our separate ways tomorrow when we get to the city. I need to do laundry, get on the Internet, refill my food supply, and get a shower, so I will hit up a hiker-friendly hostel called Garrison House, which I have heard good things about.

The wind in the trees is as sweet as music, and I feel completely content with each breath.

June 2

Good "nero" today (nero = nearly zero miles hiked in a day, usually means ten miles or less). Backflip, Patches, and I enjoyed an easy ten-mile hike to the other side of Bear Mountain, where the AT met up with the city and I bade good-bye to my friends. On the way to the Garrison House, I ran into some other hikers who stayed in Fort Montgomery last night at the Holiday Inn Express. As I made my way through town for the first time, I hear catcalls and wolf whistles: I looked farther down the street and saw I was being beckoned by the Fellowship. As I approached, I recognized all the familiar faces: Treebeard, Stormsong, Pants, Niners, Katmandu, and Stillwater. Our timing was perfect, as we were all in the mood for something to eat; so before they left town, we ate lunch together. I like these people. After we agreed to keep an eye out for each other on the trail, I made my way to the cozy and comfortable Garrison House, where I took a shower and have been doing laundry.

This place is one of the most welcoming places I have ever been to; I appear to be the only guest here. I'm relaxing in the living room of a manor house that was built in 1751, shamelessly wearing a bath towel while I wait for my clothes to finish drying. I just might have the place to myself tonight. More than any other place, this hostel has made me feel at home because of the comfortable surroundings and the pictures on the wall, which remind me of those I have in my own house. I felt happy to be on this adventure, but I missed home at the same time. All this relaxing today will fuel a great day of hiking tomorrow.

I am less than eight hundred miles from Katahdin now, and that means I might be making that final summit in the last week of July. The idea that I will find myself there fills me with more excitement than I know what to do with, and I want to scream with delight.

June 4

The last two days have been sensational. I left the town of Fort Montgomery yesterday morning at about 9:00 a.m. and enjoyed another day of perfect New York weather and terrain. As far as actually hiking, this has been my favorite state so far. Five miles along the trail, I came across a gas station mini-mart, which was equipped with a fully stocked Boar's Head delicatessen, where I ordered an excellent sub sandwich. I was suitably impressed by the flat-screen television in the men's room; I had never seen that kind of extravagance in a gas station bathroom before.

I hiked with passion yesterday, full of energy and happy to do the twenty-five miles to the RPH Shelter. It was an excellent decision. On the way to the shelter I crossed paths with a few hikers that I hadn't seen since my first week on the trail, including Spam, Face and Sensei. It had been a month and a half since I last saw these guys, so they barely recognized me. In that time I had learned to hike faster, switched out my gear, grown a beard, and lost whatever excess fat I had on my body. I passed them after a brief chat because I didn't want to kill my momentum, and they were headed to the same shelter anyway. Once I got to the shelter, I was positively stunned by all who were there: the Fellowship, the Corsican (who I last saw before Easter), and Riverguide.

It was a reunion of the ages, and it wasn't even planned. The shelter and grassy campgrounds provided ample room for all of us to spread out and sleep for the night after we ate heartily and chatted about the places we had been, what we had seen, and anything else that was interesting. Everyone missed each other greatly. The guys I hadn't seen in a couple of months commented on how much of a distance hiker I had become, compared to when they met me, and it made me feel like I belonged. It was a happy night that seemed to exist outside reality.

Today, we all hiked twenty miles together to our destination: a garden center that welcomed hikers, with porch space for us to rest comfortably overnight. Spam's parents had driven from Boston with an impressive supply of hot dogs, sandwiches, fruit, sodas, and home-made cookies; we all filled our bellies with satisfaction. It was the perfect end to a perfect day of hiking with many of the best souls I had met in the AT community.

Last night the Fellowship headed to New York City for fun and sightseeing. Kevin and I reminisced about our 2007 New York trip, where we toured the city and almost got kicked out of David Letterman's audience for being slightly drunk and loud.

It was a happy morning, and the natural high of the previous evening was with us as we sallied forth. I have learned from the journals at the shelters along the trail that Squash is about sixty miles ahead of us, and I am guessing the Three Amigos are about as far behind. I am enjoying being a part of this society that is healthy, ambitious, decent, fun loving, humorous, and intelligent. This hike was a fantastic idea, and I am wondering if it is less of a once-ever adventure or if it could be the start of a new passion. Is it possible that I could make time in a year to hike the southern part of the AT from Catawba? Could I ever make the improbable decision to hike other long-distance trails like I have heard others do? I am filled with ideas that never crossed my mind before, and I'd better focus on completing this one before I get ahead of myself.

I can confidently say that the night all of us rendezvoused at the RPH Shelter was a ridiculously joyful evening. It was great to see Kevin again, and he was amazed at how much distance I had covered while he was off trail. Many of us hadn't seen each other in weeks, and the unanticipated reunion was an occasion we still talk about, even now. That night Sensei coined the term the Windscreen effect, *which is defined as meeting a hiker who looks to be overwhelmed and wet behind the ears, only to cross paths with him or her weeks later to find the hiker is as lean and mean as any thru-hiker on the trail (at least I think that is how* Webster's *defines the term).*

It was at the RPH shelter that I began to seriously consider hiking the southern section of the AT that I skipped. All thru-hikers that started the trail at Springer told me how gorgeous the Smoky Mountains are, and I really ought to complete the AT. I took their advice to heart.

June 6

(morning)
Had a comfortable night's sleep on a La-Z-Boy on the nursery porch yesterday before hiking eighteen miles north to the shelter. Today we crossed into the next state: Connecticut. Although the weather has stayed bright and dry, the terrain resembles the rockiness of Pennsylvania. I always love crossing state borders; it is a tangible sign of accomplishment. Last night, Corsican, Spam, Face, and I went into Kent for an evening bathed in beer, basketball, and food prepared in a kitchen by other people. The server was kind enough to get us a round on the house, which was more than welcome. I used to think that being dirty, smelly, and disheveled wouldn't attract the best out of other people, but on the AT, I couldn't be more wrong. We left the bar before midnight and slept in our tents to keep the hungry bugs away so we could sleep in peace.

I need to go into Kent again today, so I can replace my shoes, and I might as well get a good breakfast while I'm there. The Vasques that I got in Waynesboro have been great, but the miles have worn the soles away to flat, slippery bottoms. In addition to getting new shoes, I'm in need of a food resupply before I head back out onto the AT. Feeling great about everything.

(evening)
What a pleasant Connecticut day. I woke up at 8:00 a.m., packed up everything, left the campsite, and went back into Kent with Kevin at 9:00 a.m. I ate a heavenly egg-white omelet filled with salmon, red onions, and Swiss cheese and accompanied with equally excellent cups of coffee. After we stocked up on our food for the next few days, we agreed to slow down and enjoy the remainder of the day. I think it is more of an effort for me to relax than it is for Kevin, so I appreciate his tempo. I would hate to rush through this hike for the sake of mileage and miss out on the many beautiful things and places that deserve my time and attention. From that perspective, I was content

to hike just seven miles to the next camping spot. During my walk around Kent, I found a delightful bookstore called House of Books and spent an hour inside combing through the titles. I had missed the scent of paper, and I enjoyed the singular comfort that I get only from books. I bought Richard Dawkins's book *The Greatest Show on Earth*; if I'm lucky, the book will be as memorable as the day that I found it. I found a small, but suitable outfitter where I purchased a pair of Merrell trail runners, and I was elated to discover that they were *amazing* to hike in. I had my first ice cream since the half-gallon challenge, and it was as good as I hoped it would be. After one last look at the main street of Kent, I went to Tucker's Tap Room and had a few pretrail beers with Face, Sensei, and Spam. I jumped back onto the trail at 4:00 p.m. and actually enjoyed the steep climbs and sharp descents that came my way. I'm looking forward to another cocooned slumber inside my tent tonight before the twenty-two mile hike we have planned for tomorrow. I like hanging out with Kevin and our new friends; it is a nonstop party. The end of the hike actually hit me today as a goal that will come to me sooner than I am expecting, and I think that everyone else in the group feels the same way. We are all positively upbeat, and I don't think it is because of the beer (well, not completely, anyway.

June 7

Less than seven hundred miles left until I summit Katahdin; it wasn't that long ago I wrote that I had eight hundred to go. It might seem like a lot to go, but I am undaunted. In fact, the time is going by even quicker than I'd like. Today's twenty-two miles began at 7:00 a.m., and the first ten miles passed by me in just four hours, despite the challenging terrain. I rewarded myself with a three-hour break at a shelter along the way and took a well-earned nap. I read some of Richard Dawkins's book and chatted about evolution and its social implications with Sensei for a couple of hours. I chuckled to think that we were two microscopic expressions of the universe wondering about itself. Kevin got a late start to the day as usual and arrived at the shelter just as I was getting packed up to rejoin the trail. I haven't seen him since midday, and now I am resting at the agreed-upon shelter at 9:00 p.m. I expect he decided to stealth camp somewhere and will catch up to the rest of us tomorrow. In the morning, I will hike to the next shelter and wait for him there. The mosquitoes are out in force at this campsite, so it is another good night to sleep in the tent. It is a unanimous decision, since no one wants to fight mosquitoes in their sleep. Tomorrow we will cross into Massachusetts; once again another state bites the dust. I should write or call Mom soon before she files another missing person's report with the Appalachian Trail Center in Harpers Ferry. I wish I didn't have the stress of her constant worry.

June 8

Today was an easy seventeen-mile day. We took a four-hour break in the town of Salisbury, which offered plenty of coffee and a salmon bagel for breakfast (is there a breakfast more perfect than a salmon bagel?), which made for an even more enjoyable morning. I took time at the library, which happened to be the very first public library in America. Afterward, I purchased what was advertised as a powerful bug-repellent bandanna, but the bugs weren't affected in the slightest by the self-proclaimed miracle.

After town, I ascended the toughest climb of the trail so far, or so it felt; it was definitely the toughest climb since Virginia. Face, Sensei, and Spam and I ceremoniously crossed into a new state together today. Spam actually cheered when he stepped into his home state of Massachusetts. I took a picture with my cell phone and uploaded it directly to Facebook, thanks to the surprisingly strong signal at the mountaintop. It was my first AT picture to be posted for all my friends and relatives to see, and there were instant comments and likes. I didn't tell Facebook I was going on this hike, so I was interested to see how most of my friends would react to seeing Windscreen for the first time. Windscreen looks a lot like Chris, just with thicker calves, a lighter chest, and an untamed beard.

There are two shelters just 0.1 miles away from each other, and I am staying at the one just barely farther north with Spam, while Sensei and Face stay at the other. The two of us have been talking movies, songs, soundtracks, hikers, and, of course, the trail. Although Spam is fifteen years younger than me, he is easy to laugh and joke with. On the AT, everyone is a friend. We both got to our shelter mere minutes before the rain started, and it has been coming down hard for the last hour. It is definitely a great night to sleep in a shelter instead of a tent. It just occurred to me: all the nights I slept in Connecticut were inside my tent. I haven't seen Kevin all day, but he texted me to say that he was camping out just five miles south from where I am right now. Tomorrow might be a twenty-two mile day, so I will get some good sleep tonight.

June 9

With Kevin confirmed to be staying at Glen Brook five miles south of here, I wrote a letter and left it in a Ziploc bag, with his name in *big* letters, on a fence post that was on the trail path, held in place by a rock. There is no way for him to miss it. I wrote that I would just hike seventeen miles today in the hope he would catch up to me. I miss my friend.

By 1:00 p.m., a storm moved in quickly and made the sky look as if it were already evening; it was so gloomy overhead. The lightning and thunder came loudly and suddenly, and there was no shelter from any of it. I passed broken tree branches and dodged falling limbs as I pressed on in soaking wet shoes, always wondering if my pack's contents were still dry. I descended the last mountain of the day and took special care not to slip and bust my ass, which I almost did a dozen times. My glasses were wet and fogged up, but I paid attention to the blazes and kept my head about me. I had a feeling all my friends stopped at the last shelter I passed before the storm became worse, but I wasn't about to turn around; forward was the only direction I wanted to go. At the bottom of the mountain, the AT came to a paved road, and I breathed with relief; I was literally out of the woods. I had heard about a nearby hiker hostel and spontaneously decided to find my way there and get out of the storm. I caught a ride with a friendly couple who knew where the hostel was, and they were happy to save me a two-mile hike and get me to the hostel much sooner than if I had walked. I was in no mood to argue their kindness; it was another instance where my gratitude weighed just as much as my benefactors' generosity. I am glad to finally be warm, dry, clean, full, and eager to slip into a deep sleep; the storm exhausted me. I keep looking out for Kevin, both online and out the window, but there is no sign of him. I haven't seen him in two days; I hope he isn't offended by my urge to hike these distances. I will hike twenty-two miles to Upper Goose Pond Cabin tomorrow, where I will have a feeling I will see some familiar faces. The place is rumored to offer free breakfast and coffee, and that is a powerful beacon to follow.

June 10
I left the retreat center at 7:30 a.m. and found the AT around 8:15 a.m. It was drizzling all morning, and no drivers were tempted to offer a hiker a ride to the trailhead. I kept my eyes open for other hikers, but saw no one for a long time. I churned out twenty-two miles entirely without a single break; the siren song of Upper Goose Pond Cabin was that compelling. When I arrived at my destination, I found Face already there resting inside the cabin, and Sensei arrived not an hour after I did. None of us knew or had heard anything about Spam or Riverguide). I took a much-needed dip in Goose Pond and rinsed away the day's sweat; even in such a wet climate, hiking several miles can break a sweat. On the island in the middle of the pond, I found the Corsican basking in his underwear, soaking up what sunshine began to break through the clouds. French people always seem to be at their happiest in their underwear, I've noticed.

I will continue hiking tomorrow, but I have accepted that I must take a zero so that Kevin can catch up to me. I wouldn't be so occupied if he kept up with me, but I know that he likes his pace. I don't mind our pacing differences, but I think we are going to have to agree to hike our own hikes so we can both get what we want from this experience. I think I will go seventeen miles tomorrow with Face and Sensei and look for Tom Levardi's place in Dalton with them. We have heard from multiple sources that he welcomes hikers into his home and loves to cook huge meals for his guests.

Taking a zero actually sounds pretty great. I have a package to pick up from Mom in Cheshire, and I hope to find a theater so I can watch *X-Men: First Class*. I had thought to hike the entire trail without seeing any movies, but this one looks so damn good, I am breaking my pointless rule.

This cabin at Upper Goose Pond is the coziest dormitory I have ever seen, and it is packed with hikers of all sorts. Whether it is because of the generosity of the cabin itself, or because of the recent bad weather, everyone is happy to be here tonight. The cabin is enclosed by a screen that denies bugs entry, so we are free to play games, drink, eat, and read our books without being molested. I am going to sleep like a coma patient tonight; it feels good to be reunited with friends after the threatening storm. I trust that I will see Kevin soon, too, and he will, no doubt, be just as happy to see me.

June 12

Yesterday morning all twelve of us who stayed at the cabin were woken up by the caretaker who announced there were pancakes and coffee waiting for us downstairs. It was all we could do to not scramble out of our beds and run downstairs like children on Christmas morning. There were huge dinner plates stacked with fluffy pancakes, bottles of Vermont syrup, juices, milk, and what appeared to be an unending flow of hot coffee. We all ate with gusto and then packed up everything with spirit as Sensei sang verse after verse of "Big Rock Candy Mountain." Nothing could have invigorated me better than that amazing breakfast, and I was raring to get started on the twenty-one-mile hike. Good people accompanied me all day, with either Face, Sensei, or both of them, and we crossed the miles in awe of the beauty, the memory of the cabin, or thoughts of what was to come. Although rain greeted us early in the day, it didn't last long; the weather stayed cool and cloudy all day, which kept the bugs to a minimum.

About halfway through the day, Sensei asked me if the hike had changed me in any way, and I had to take some time to think about my answer. After a while, I told him that on the AT I found people who think and live like I do, and the consistent health and happiness of the people around me have peeled away many layers of hardened cynicism. This is something that I want to keep in my life: a culture that is happy, healthy, ambitious, humorous, and idealistic. I haven't surrounded myself with so many positive people in my life before. As I explained this to him, I realized how much better my life could be if I associated with traveling, nonconformist cultures like this one. Surely there are other places where I can find other groups of like-minded souls; I should seriously consider finding jobs that attract people like these from now on, instead of money-obsessed people who are too focused on acquiring possessions and conforming to thoughtlessness.

Last night the three of us found the well-reputed "Tom's place" in Dalton and had our expectations blown completely away. We had planned to make our camp on a patch of grass or porch space if we were lucky. Instead, we were welcomed to shower, wash our clothes, sleep on mattresses, and coordinate rides into town. A few other hikers were there and assured us this place was the most difficult place to hike away from; we would do well to rest and wait for our friends here. Before we had a chance to discuss it together, we individually decided to take a zero at Tom's place to catch up on sleep and savor the feeling of being dry and warm. I had never before seen such a display of gracious selflessness as I did at Tom's place. Last night we cleaned up and got our stuff dried and then went to have our fill of beer and damn good Massachusetts cooking. It was a peaceful night that sat well with all of us.

This morning I tried eggs Florentine for the first time; it might just be my new favorite breakfast dish. Tom gave us a ride to the supermarket so Face, Sensei, and I could stock up from a wide selection of food, and afterward I asked to be dropped off at the movie theater. No one else cared to see a movie, so I went solo. I was entertained not only by one of the best movies I saw that year, but was pleasantly wrapped in synthetic comfort and silence; the kind that doesn't exist in nature.

Last night, Yikes and Thru showed up just before dinnertime, and then Challenger showed up a little later with Corsican; it was a happy reunion for all of us. I heard nothing from Kevin, so I decided to wait one more day at Tom's. Even though we filled his house with hikers, he was eager for us to stay and rest as long as we needed or wanted without the slightest concern that we might be overstaying. Tom reminded us that giving our bodies rest was just as important as exercise itself, and I had to admit that another day off might be a very good idea. I thanked him profusely, and I even discreetly left some money for him in an envelope by his bedroom door, but he quietly found me and returned it. He assured me that providing a haven for us hikers was his pleasure and that my gratitude was more than enough. I was beside myself with admiration for this man.

It had been several days since I saw Kevin, so I was happy for the opportunity to wait for him there. Hiking is an indescribable adventure, but taking time away from the trail from time to time is a delight as well. My scabs, scratches, and bruises from tackling the AT are healing noticeably, and my skin is reveling in the mosquito-less breeze. Surprisingly, my time in Dalton has given me the opportunity to view the long-distance hiking tradition through Tom's eyes. I picked up the box of goodies Mom sent me and ate most of it since many of the items would be too heavy to take on the trail with me, but they went well with the movie instead. I am 619 miles away from Katahdin, and the distance isn't as intimidating as I feel it should be. Face bought his plane ticket to North Carolina, thereby establishing his deadline and, by proxy, possibly mine to reach the northern terminus (since I intend to hike with these guys until the end). Rather than feeling any kind of stress, I am filled with excitement. I need to consider getting my own plane tickets soon, but I have some time before I need to fear rising ticket prices. The end is in sight, but still distant.

June 14

Face, Sensei, and I took two zeros at Tom's place. As we sat down to eat Tom's spaghetti at his picnic table last night, several hikers showed up with wide smiles and dirty appearances, just like we did. Among the group were Kevin and Spam, so the evening exploded into a frenzy of relief, jocularity, and furious storytelling. After Kevin and I told each other our tales of the last week, he brought up what was on both of our minds. He admitted that he wasn't interested in hiking the kind of miles that I was. I had a feeling he might say that; the conversation was a happy one, without disappointment. He didn't want me to slow down, and I didn't want him to hike faster or longer just because I did. We agreed to hike our own hikes and promptly got down to the business of enjoying our last evening in Dalton. It was a happy suggestion to hike independently, and we drank to our decision at the bar down the street from Tom's.

I was relieved that I was now free to hike big miles, and Kevin was probably just as pleased to be untethered to me. The beers flowed last night as our huge group talked about the futility of politics and watched a hockey game on TV. Just like the hikers who left before us warned me, this is the hardest place I have had to say good-bye to thus far. I assume this will be the last time I see Kevin for a while, which sucks; I know our friendship is intact, no matter how many months or years pass until we get to clink beers again. I asked Spam, Face, and Sensei if I could officially join their group, and of course they all said I could. We all hike the same pace and are excellent company together, so it makes sense. I need to get my stuff packed up and get going. It is drizzling outside, and the more hours I spend here, the more tempted I am to stay another night. I want to hike twenty miles, and it is already 9:30 a.m. I am enjoying hanging out with all these hikers exchanging stories and anecdotes, but the trail isn't going to hike itself!

Oh, now I have to wonder if Dalton wasn't in fact the best part of my northbound AT hike. I remember with unblemished fondness the wonderfully quaint town of Dalton, the interaction between so many hikers, and the chance to recuperate in comfort while it blustered incessantly outside. It was such a joy to see Kevin again after a few days where we were incommunicado and separated by miles and rainstorms. Our decision to hike our own hikes was a good idea, and our friendship hasn't suffered a bit; we are still great friends to this day.

I'll never stop admiring trail angels like Tom Levardi. This amazing man even went so far as to have the trail route go down the street that his house is on just so hikers could more easily stay at his place. It was obvious to anyone who met him that he loved giving to the community and would never accept anything but our thanks in return. When I think of people in my life that I should emulate more, Tom is always among them.

June 15

It was insanely difficult to walk away from Tom's house yesterday, but we did. I like hiking with these guys because we are always eager to cross the same miles, take the same breaks, and talk about interesting things. We hiked seventeen miles yesterday and crashed for the night at the unexpected shelter at the top of Mount Greylock. It was a fully enclosed shelter, and it offered more than enough room for the four of us. That evening, the rain cleared just before sunset, allowing the most dazzling view of the evening sky we had seen in what felt like ages. I woke up this morning and savored the sunrise in solitude and ate breakfast quietly before anyone else woke up. The memory of Tom's place is warm in my heart, but the stark serenity of unblemished nature stirs something deep inside me unlike anything else. The high elevation makes it a chilly morning, but I will warm up soon, once I get hiking. I don't want to put on my wet socks and shoes, but I must. The goal is to hike to Bennington, about twenty-three miles away from here, and into Vermont. Today marks my second full month on the AT; just five or six weeks left.

June 16

Yesterday was a fun hike with Sensei, Face, and Spam, but twenty-one miles of hiking in soggy socks and thoroughly mud-wet shoes gave me top-of-the-toe blisters that were impossible to ignore. The blisters forced me to stop at the shelter just four miles south of Bennington, as the others continued all the way into town to watch the hockey game. As it turned out, that was the best decision I could have made; my blisters were extremely raw and red, so I needed to allow time for them to heal. This morning I hiked those four miles in near agony, but was relieved by the short distance. I hitchhiked into town effortlessly enough thanks to a kind driver and walked up to the Autumn Inn where my friends had arranged to stay. We ate breakfast together at the Blue Benn Café, and I considered taking a day off my feet and soaking them in salt water to expedite the healing process. Word had it that The Vortex was a hostel that offered work-for-stays for hikers, so I made plans to stay there for a night. I met my hosts and took up their offer of a bicycle so I could ride back to the Autumn Inn to inform Spam, Sensei, and Face I would catch up to them after my feet healed.

The day was warm and bright, and the chill of the last couple of nights disappeared along with the caked blood and dirt. To celebrate arriving in Vermont, I treated myself to a pint of Ben & Jerry's Half Baked ice cream before getting to my work-for-stay: dusting the music room in Chris and Arla's house. For dinner I ate a huge burger at the local brewery and walked around the small town in sandals. This place is friendly, cozy, and as inviting as Dalton, but with its own character. I am glad I got to spend some time here.

June 17

I opted to take a zero today and let my feet heal completely. I was eager to get back out on the trail and try to catch up to the others, but to do so would have been impetuous and silly. Foot care is a priority, and I had to obey sensibility. I ate breakfast at Isabella's Café and read my Richard Dawkins book on The Vortex's wraparound porch. When I heard approaching voices, I got up to see who it was: who else but Challenger, Corsican, Herb, Spice, and Kevin! It was a carefree day spent watching a parade of classic cars drive through town while we ate pints of Ben & Jerry's ice cream. We all agreed to eat dinner and sample beers at the same brewery I enjoyed last night. Outside, I noticed a dazzling beauty in a low-cut blue dress and a sash that read "Miss Vermont" in huge letters, so I decided I'd meet her. She flashed one of those practiced beauty queen smiles for our picture: she in her gorgeous dress and I in my trail-stained shirt and sporting a wildly unkempt beard. It rained all afternoon and evening, with plenty of lightning and thunder, too. Fortunately, the barn we are all staying in behind The Vortex is roomy and well built, so we want for nothing. My toes feel like they are healed enough to resume the hike tomorrow, so I will. I hope little injuries like this will not be common between here and Katahdin; I have eyes for a July summit.

June 18

I'm back, baby! I hiked twenty miles today, and my feet have never felt better. I left Bennington this morning at 10:30 a.m. (after a great breakfast and a phone chat with Mom). Halfway through the day, I ran into Treebeard and Stillwater who were taking a little break along the trail. It was good to chat with them, but my legs didn't want to stop, so I continued on without delay. There was thunder in the distance that I was afraid would be followed by a great storm, but I was thankfully wrong. There was just a thirty-minute shower, which was actually pleasantly refreshing. I spent the day considering all the options I am presented with in my life: to go to college (which will happen after the trail); to teach English overseas after my degree is in hand; to be an aviation contractor (which would make use of my air force experience); to sell my house and everything in it in order to live a simple, untethered life; or to get a combat-zone job so that I can pay off the house in about two years. I have to acknowledge how fortunate I am to have many choices; I want to make good use of the next two years so I can make the best decision. It gives me a sense of safety, not to mention success, to have these options.

Tomorrow I will hike twenty-four miles because I want to catch up to Sensei, Face, and Spam. If I put on some speed, I just might catch up to them in the next week. I hope I have seen the last of my injuries, and I wouldn't be upset if I went the rest of the way without any more crippling blisters. I have been spared giardia and Lyme's disease thus far, so I will keep on being watchful of my surroundings and careful about what I drink. I expect the next six weeks to go by quickly, so I am taking extra care to enjoy the trail and to live in the moment. It isn't often I get to accomplish a thing like this, and I don't want to be complacent about any of it. I intend to enjoy everything that the hike brings my way, if I can, and not let all this swampy mud get the best of me.

June 19

I hiked twenty-three miles today beginning at 6:00 a.m., and I expect tomorrow will be the same. Even though I'm getting proficient at hopping gracefully from rock to rock through miles of mud, I can't wait to hike on solid land again. The weather was perfect; I came across sweetly chirping birds; dozens of rivers, streams, and brooks; and a couple of lakes. I'm not sure if the bugs are less annoying, or if I'm just getting used to them as a permanent part of the hike; I haven't used my bug mask or bug repellant in weeks. I was absolutely ravenous by noon, so I devoured a bunch of snack bars and two pasta meals during my hour-long break. I need to be careful; otherwise, I'll be out of food before I make it to Hanover. I miss Kevin, and it makes me sad to think I won't see him on the AT again. I have been crossing big distances each day, so I have a feeling he is relaxing tonight many miles away from here. I have no idea when I will see him next; it may be an entirely different chapter in our lives. I chatted with Andrew today, and he pointed out that I should buy my plane ticket home before long; I might be done with this hike even sooner that I expect. I also might take some more zeroes and savor my time on the trail, so I need to give some serious thought to my departure from Maine. I should definitely have my flight booked in two weeks, wherever I will be by then.

June 21

What an awesome couple of days I've had. I planned to hike 23 miles yesterday from the Bromley Shelter, but I was motivated to go to the Clarendon Shelter, making it a trek of 31.4 miles. I finally broke into the thirties, and I was exhausted. I am in love with Vermont. The mud is becoming less bothersome with reduced rain, and these mountain peaks offer the most gorgeous vistas I have seen in ages. I am intoxicated by the cool breezes, alpine scents, and crisp air; this is hiking at its best. Today I hiked twenty-two miles and I feel exhilarated. The special thing about today was that I hiked naked. *Naked!* Twenty of those miles were bare assed, and I have to say that I loved it. On the first day of summer it is a tradition for hikers to shed their inhibitions; I'd never get a better opportunity to do so than here and now. Hike Naked Day began early for me, and I set off from my shelter before 7:00 a.m. It was a little brisk, and I didn't want to be breaking fresh trail cobwebs with my more sensitive body parts, so I hiked in clothes for the first hour of the day. Around 8:30 a.m. I took my first break. I ate breakfast, replenished my water supply, and stripped. I folded my shirt and shorts and kept them at my side for quick access for any number of reasons that might have come up. I made my way wearing only my shoes, socks, and bandanna (on my head). To indulge tradition and disregard dignity, even if it was for just one day, was absolutely liberating. An hour after I noticed how incredibly liberating hiking this way was, I met a couple of older hikers coming from the opposite direction. Judging from the way they avoided eye contact and barely acknowledged my chipper good morning, it was obvious they wanted nothing to do with whatever I was all about. Twice, the AT intersected highways, so I would hang back until I could cross between speeding cars, then dash across all the lanes as fast as I could. I can only imagine what I looked like sprinting nude with my trekking poles (and everything else) swinging wildly. Sophisticated, no doubt! Before the end of my nude hike, I turned a corner and saw a family that was out for a jaunt. They had noticed me first, and the father kept his young daughter facing his belly as I passed them with embarrassment.

"Oh, I'm so sorry!" I exclaimed with heartfelt regret at intruding upon their wholesome family outing.

"Don't be. I think it's great!" the mom said. It was clear she was all about hiker tradition and had been enjoying the events of the day. "Let your freak flag fly!"

I let out an audible sigh of relief. "Thanks for not making me feel like a pervert."

I noticed the father wasn't keen on conversing with me, but not in a negative way. He seemed to just wish he knew beforehand what kind of craziness was in store for him when he agreed to hike the AT section near his house. That situation could have gone any number of worse ways, and I'm glad that it didn't. Sometimes when I think the United States is too wound up or too conservative (as the media so often portrays), I think of the first day of summer on the AT and rest easy knowing that at least one group of people are marching to the beat of their own drum.

When the sun sank toward the horizon, I decided to get dressed. I stopped at a gas station where I refilled my bottle of denatured alcohol and ate a roast beef and Swiss cheese hoagie. Not long after I ate, I noticed an outfitter with a large covered porch and outlets to charge my electronic devices. This is a perfect place to cowboy camp and reflect on the hike. I am prepared to fall asleep early tonight so I can get up and go at daybreak tomorrow. I am shooting for twenty-seven miles tomorrow, and the day after that I just might be able to find my hiking buddies in Hanover!

Before the first day of summer, I made use of the Internet to see whether hiking nude was even legal and was encouraged by what I read. It so happens that in the state of Vermont, it is perfectly legal to be out in public without a stitch of clothing on, just as long as no inappropriate touching of self was happening. I decided that I could keep from playing with myself for a day and get a full-body tan. I knew that if I didn't, I would regret it; it isn't often that I am allowed to hang out nude all day, and it sounded like fun. It was fun. *I recommend it to anyone who wants to savor true freedom.*

June 22

I enjoyed a sheltered sleep on the outfitter deck that overlooked a tree-filled valley typical of Vermont. I woke up with the kind of energy that belongs to a younger person, and as much exuberance. I woke up at 4:30 a.m. since I went to sleep pretty early and was beating feet on the trail an hour later, my earliest morning departure yet. I was determined to catch up with Spam, who I could tell was just ten miles ahead of me by the pattern of his journal entries at the last few shelters as well as words from slower hikers who we have both been passing. If I'm lucky, I'll catch up with Face and Sensei who were around these parts just two days ago. With my friends as motivation, I hiked twenty-seven miles to this shelter for the night. I caught up to Pleasure earlier today, a thru-hiker I met at Tom Levardi's hiker house in Dalton back in Massachusetts. He mentioned that I just missed seeing Spam by a mere hour from the shelter I took my first break at, and we hiked on from there with the intention of catching up with my friend. We enjoyed a full eleven hours of conversation as we covered the fields, mud, rain, and rocks to get where we were going. Pleasure is as easygoing as his hiker name implied, and the miles flew. We took lunch at a rickety wooden tower that appeared to be held intact more by my fear of falling than by nails and bolts. I wolfed down the last of my Cabot cheese, which I am insanely fond of, and Pleasure filled up on his gorp (good ol' raisins and peanuts). We felt the first few raindrops of a storm, which persisted all day, but we remained fleet of foot throughout the last fourteen miles of heavy downpour. We were soaked through to our souls—and made do with drenched shirts, shorts, socks, and shoes—but in high spirits. Days like today add character that color the beauty and warmth of better days, so I appreciated wiping the fog from my glasses every few minutes and taking care not to fall across the slick rocks and let the upbeat conversations distract me from the chilly gusts that filled that latter half of today. When we got to the shelter, I looked forward especially to surprising Spam, who had no idea I had put on speed to close up to his location; doing this was more exciting to me than getting into dry clothes and wrapping myself up like a burrito inside my sleeping bag. When I turned the corner to enter the shelter, I heard his familiar voice shout out in mad disbelief "Windscreen?" It was almost an echo of his reaction to seeing me again in New York weeks ago. We were wiped out from navigating through the rain-filled miles but fell asleep knowing we were going to see our other friends tomorrow in Hanover. It will be just a fourteen-mile jaunt—small potatoes compared to what we had become accustomed to of late. We chatted about the possibility of taking a zero there if we can find Sensei and Face; it feels like we have earned one.

June 24

We made it to Hanover yesterday! It was a delightful hike through wet trails and dripping branches, but being around friends made it seem like sunshine, and when we approached the Dartmouth-ruled town of Hanover, we couldn't have been more thrilled. It only takes a few days of wilderness and constant dampness to be shown how marvelous enclosed, climate-controlled buildings are, especially when they offer discounted pizzas to long-distance hikers passing through. When we arrived, Spam and I turned on our phones and were greeted with amazing reception. Both of us had waiting texts that told us where to find Face and Sensei, so we made our way there via the commuter bus that ran around town. We knocked loudly on the hotel room door, and a reunion of smiles and laughter ensued. We all commented how each of us assumed that we wouldn't meet up as a group ever again, and we couldn't have been happier to be proven wrong. We all agreed to take a zero tomorrow, since we have just 450 miles left to our hike and the end is not far off. We have the White Mountains coming up soon, and they are reputed to be as difficult to overcome as they are amazing to behold. It is the perfect mix of intimidation and guarantee of reward that fills any hiker with the passion to continue; it is why I think we have all pushed through the insane challenges of this insanely long hike.

Hanover is quite possibly the best town I have seen on the AT. It is hiker friendly, well groomed, and collegiate and offers free public transportation. Today and yesterday have been a much-needed respite, like every zero that I have taken on the AT. Dry feet are a welcome change of pace (no pun intended), and warm pizza fills my belly and swims with cold delicious beer. As if realized from a dream, I found out that a place called Lou's Café offered free slices of pie to hikers like me. I couldn't believe it was happening, but the slice of strawberry-rhubarb pie didn't lie as I gave it a happy home. Every yummy dish will fuel me to power up and down the imposing peaks and ridges of the Presidential Range of the Whites. I wonder how I will feel in a week, when I am on the other side of the most physically demanding terrain of the AT. Sensei keeps telling me how surprised he was to see me arrive here; they had no idea they'd see me again. I feel like a truly seasoned hiker, and I wonder if this is the start of a deeper passion as opposed to a onetime adventure. I could see myself doing more of these, and maybe I will make time to hike the southern third of the AT next year. I think I'd like that tremendously.

June 25

Last night the four of us crashed in the hotel room we shared and watched movies until we passed out. The comfort of mattresses, blankets, proper pillows, nearby running water and a bathroom, warm pizza, cold beer, and zero bugs made the mediocre motel room good enough for royalty, at least in our eyes. This morning we were ready to put comfortable Hanover behind us and cover some miles. We have a ready-for-the-Whites attitude, and although we didn't get back on the trail until 11:00 a.m., we all had eager cadences.

"Crush beer, crush can, crush miles," Face uttered as he got started on his tallboy, intending to draw magnificent hiking power from the beer goodness. We hiked seventeen miles that were rarely silent. The troop was back and ready to rock. I still missed hiking with Kevin; it would have been perfect to summit Katahdin with him. I wondered where he might be.

Every time I think that I will be at that terminal summit, I feel giddy, and I convert that excitement into hiking power. I know the hardest part is still ahead, but there just doesn't seem to be any fear about it. I asked Spam if he minded me catching a ride with him and his family from Maine to Boston and then flying back home to Albuquerque from there. He assured me that no one would mind, but he would ask them first before he committed to it. The more I see the profile of the peaks ahead, the more I want to conquer them. Bring it on!

June 26

Not a bad day, overall. It was a little frustrating having to deal with constant wet, rooted trails and dozens of mud pits, but I must admit I am used to it by now. The worst part is the mud that manages to get inside my shoes and socks, creating top-of-the-toe blisters again, which are definitely unwelcome at this point in the hike. The breezes after the laborious climbs are delicious rewards, and I savor every gentle trace of them on my neck, face, arms, and legs. Today was an easy nineteen-mile day, and my blisters didn't pose the handicap that I was worried about. I left ahead of the other three because I knew they would catch up to me before midday. I pressed through the first twelve miles without a break and then took a long one at a cool hexagonal shelter and flipped through the journal to see where the other hikers I knew might be. It is a great routine of powerful exercise and gentle relaxation in between. I like this hiking gig.

June 27

I loved today. Even though I was a little worried about my tender toes, I happily hiked fifteen miles. The muddy, but easy morning led us to a hiker-friendly hostel, where the four of us took a lunch break. We ate microwave pizzas and ice-cream sandwiches and drank sodas as we watched *The Big Lebowski* on the host's television. The best thing that happened that afternoon was drying my socks and shoes in the warm sunlight, which made the rest of the day's hiking a delight. Leaving the hostel was difficult, but not as bad as it could have been because we were all determined to summit Mount Moosilauke today. It was indeed a challenge, but not quite the overbearing obstacle I was bracing myself for. It turned out to be a refreshing climb, and I kept up with Spam for most of it, even at his long-strided quick pace. I will never in my life forget how exhilarating it was to break the tree line and be treated with the pure, high-altitude air, alpine-like smell, and unbearably spectacular panorama of the surrounding mountains. We all took a break for about an hour and a half and watched the sun set gracefully, as if it were a show directed only for us on this lone mountaintop. We acknowledged that this would be the pace for the next week: insane climbs rewarded by heavenly vistas. It was good to be here; I was happy to feel alive.

June 29

Holy hell, yesterday was *tough*. My attitude stayed good all morning, all through the full descent of Moosilauke, even though it took two hours to descend just a mile and a half. The six-mile stretch from the foot of Moosilauke to the shelter where I took my lunch break was exhausting beyond belief. There were endless obstacles comprised of rocks, closely growing trees, jerky ups and downs, mud slips, and not a single vista that opened up to the sky or the forest that I was navigating through. It was difficult to keep a standard pace, and I was constantly shifting my feet, as if awkwardly dancing just to keep going forward. Face caught up to me and was equally discouraged by the slow mileage we were suffering through. Fortunately, it got better in the afternoon. We were relieved to summit a mountain in the early evening and see the open sky, even though it was sunless and blustery. Face noticed that his guidebook mentioned we were close to a well-reputed hiker hostel owned by veteran hiker Chet, and the thought of proper sleep and town facilities was more than tempting for all of us. It was sorely painful to pass the first work-for-stay hut, but the reward would be Chet's place, we agreed. We were joined by Yikes, who I had crossed paths with a couple of times earlier in Vermont and New Hampshire, and invited her to join our merry band, if only just for a while. She admitted that she liked our group and felt safer with the bunch of us than she did on her own, so we welcomed her along. That evening we crossed through a laborious eighteen miles but were urged by the promise of all the delights any small town promises hungry hikers. There was just one place still open by the time we made it to town, but it was more than enough for our basic wants. It was so good to sink my teeth into lamb-filled gyros and slices of pizza. We plan to hike out later today after the thunderstorm passes us by. I slipped and fell more times yesterday than I think I did the whole hike before, so I suspected the cause was either my own fatigue or my disintegrating shoes. I plan to get new shoes after this journal entry is written, so I look forward to the return of fully operational feet once more. I chatted with Andrew today, and he warned me that Mom was in a bad mood, so that phone conversation should be tons of fun. Compared to family drama, hiking this trail is positively easy.

On the AT I crossed paths with so many awesome people, I couldn't possibly list all of them here. I wrote about them in my journal and managed to stay in touch with most of them for a long time, even years after our hike. Five of us stuck together the longest and summited Katahdin on the same jubilant day. Yikes, Sensei, Spam, and Face discovered that we all hiked at the same ambitious pace, didn't like to distract ourselves off the trail too much (until the final couple of weeks, anyway), and got along well with each other, even after the most trying of days. At thirty-eight, I was the oldest member of our group, and at twenty years old, Spam was the youngest and most familiar with hiking. He was equal parts laughter and energy, always motivating each of us to devour bigger miles. He and I laughed, sang, and idly chitchatted the miles away, day after day. He taught me everything I never wanted to know about Justin Bieber. Face was a welcome source of cynicism, dark humor, and a hard edge that tempered well against the giddy laughter and lofty attitudes that characterized the rest of us. Our close ages and military backgrounds made for a common ground that supported us during our most exhausting frustrations, and we put away more than a few pitchers of beer during our rests from the AT. Sensei was the first ethnomusicologist I ever met, and his passion for all things cultural and musical didn't disappoint me. I have met so few people who share my intense love of cinema music, but Sensei more than held his own in our discussions of movie compositions from the '70s and on. Who knows how many miles flew past us as we went on about the genius of James Horner, Hanz Zimmer, Alan Silvestri, Jerry Goldsmith, and, of course, John Williams. Yikes was the much-needed beautiful girl of the crew and was, according to Face, "as comfortable crunching beers as crunching miles." We shared endless chats about science, travels across America, and our aviation experiences. Whenever I worried too much about how tough a mountain range was, if the mosquitoes were kicking my ass, or if the weather wasn't sunny enough, Yikes would be there to tell me to "stop being such a princess."

June 30

Nineteen miles, in the Whites, in the rain, with just one trekking pole, after a spontaneous zero (due to the lingering threatening storm), the five of us bade Chet heartfelt thanks and left his house at 6:30 a.m. sharp. The weather was still horrible, but we pressed through it undaunted. We crested three peaks but couldn't see a damn thing because of the torrential rain and strong gusts that made above-tree-line hiking an extremely chilling affair. Crossing Franconia Notch and Lafayette Peak were especially miserable, and we all but sprinted to get out of the harsh elements while making sure to not lose track of the AT and get lost on the other non-AT trails that we came across. Before I could catch it, my pack cover blew into the wind, but Spam caught it right away. Sensei's blew away, too, but his disappeared into the opaque sky as he raced to get out of the freezing rain. I later gave him mine, since I lined my pack with a plastic bag, never losing my desperation to keep everything inside it dry. Spam and I hiked non-stop until we got to another hiker hut at 2:00 p.m. and took a warm lunch break inside. The potato soup was a godsend, and the peanut butter chocolate brownies were enough to sustain us for the rest of the hiking day. We continued upward for seven more miles to the next hut. Those miles were slippery, cloudy, and treacherous, but we all made it safely to that beautiful crowded hut. We were grateful to be given a roof and an enclosed space for just a night. Hiking with just one trekking pole has made me a more cautious hiker, so I think I will see how long I can go without replacing the one that broke. I haven't fallen once all day, so I just might be on to something. I fell in love with hiking through trees; they provide cover from the sheets of rain so that I can travel in relative comfort.

July 1

I am so freaking exhausted. I am immensely grateful for these well-placed huts throughout the White Mountains. We stayed at Zealand Falls Hut last night and did the dishes for everyone who stayed there in exchange for sleeping on the floor. Good trade, if you ask me. We got stepping at 9:15 a.m., and I didn't take a single break until I got to Mitzbah Hut. I got out of the sudden downpour and stayed there an hour until the sun shone. The tomato and black bean soup was just what I was craving, and I filled up on some strong black coffee there as well. By the time I set my pack on my back again, I was raring to go. From there it was just a five-mile jaunt to the Lake-in-the-Clouds Hut, where we all agreed to spend the night. It was as good as Valhalla, if I am to be honest! The weather thickened up so much that it was impossible to see farther than five feet ahead, so I was relieved to see the hut when I did; it was a welcome sign not just of warmth and shelter, but also that I hadn't wandered off the trail by accident. Even through the fog and rain, the views I beheld from the Webster and Jackson Peaks were not to be missed. I didn't stop to savor them like I would if it had been sunny, but it was still a remarkable experience. We are beginning to see the first southbounders of the year, and we talk incessantly in groups, enthusiastically sharing information, advice, and warnings about the trail ahead for both directions. We enjoyed meeting these fresh-faced southbounders who had so much of our own memories ahead of them to experience; I was actually a little envious of them. One of them was particularly friendly and funny. She went by the trail name Moose-Mulch, and it was a shame we weren't hiking the same direction. This community never ceases to entertain me at every turn. Tomorrow we are planning to hike another twenty miles and will take off early since we elected to stay in "the dungeon" for ten bucks each as opposed to staying late to make good on a work-for-stay. My good night's sleep will begin soon; I can feel it. I love the feeling of a warm and full belly, dry feet, and a room full of happy friends. It is freezing in this stone room, but our sleeping bags capture all the warmth we want.

July 3

(afternoon)
Yesterday morning was exceptional. I woke up fully rested at 4:30 a.m. and left the tiny "dungeon" where my friends and I slept for the night snugly in our cozy sleeping bags. I was immediately freezing once I rolled up my bag, but I went upstairs to the main room where dozens of other section hikers and thru-hikers were still in deep sleep. I drank some water, ate some porridge, and warmed myself with some delicious coffee from the kitchen. I saw Spam briefly before I headed out, and we agreed on the mileage we wanted to accomplish so we knew where to meet up at the end of the day. The hike began by immediately climbing Mount Washington, and as if on cue, the day broke with a spectacular sunrise as I crested the peak. Instead of rain and clouds, there was a sky bathed in unblemished sunshine that illuminated the hundreds of miles around that the summit permitted me to see. Since it was a holiday weekend, there were many more people on the trail yesterday than I have ever seen. The hike was the best experience imaginable, all the way until it was time to descend Mount Adams. The twenty-mile day we planned was cut short due to the slow-going, knee-punishing miles of the toughest downhill terrain Sensei and I had ever come across. Instead of making the final climb of the day up Wildcat Mountain with Spam and Face, the two of us elected to remain in the valley by the visitors center at Pinkham

Notch and stealth camp for the night. Sensei and I were exhausted throughout our bodies, especially our knees, and had no desire to hike the last three miles of our planned day.

Wildcat Mountain looked imposing as hell last night, but this morning it was an exhilarating challenge that posed no threat. Last night an elderly couple gave us their buffet tickets for free, and we ate generous amounts of vegetable soup, chicken curry, and Indian rice. We decided to head along the trail away from the visitors center to find a suitable place to camp before the sun disappeared. Both of us were asleep soundly before 9:00 p.m. This morning I woke up with un-bridled energy and hiked furiously up and across Wildcat Mountain until I reached the final hut in the White Mountain National Forest. When we both met up for a well-deserved break inside that shelter, we agreed to do just thirteen miles for the day, camp out on the trail tonight, and hike eight miles into Gorham tomorrow. We knew that Face and Spam would be hiking into Gorham tonight, but a slower pace with fewer miles appealed to our labored skeletons. We also had no idea where Yikes was, since the last time we saw her was yesterday morning at the Lake-in-the-Clouds Hut. I hope that she isn't lost or hurt, and I wanted her to catch up to us if she was behind us.

(evening)
It is resplendent to stay in a shelter again, after so much time in the wild forest. Sensei and I completed a comfortable fifteen-mile day with a few big climbs and descents, but nothing as formidable as Mount Adams. Today we were expecting to see thunderstorms, but we were only met with cold rain. We are dealing with wet socks and shoes again, but tomorrow we will be met by all the luxuries of a small-town respite that we could ever want. Hikers sing the praises of Gorham's hospitality and facilities, so today's discomfort is made bet-ter by the promise of tomorrow's rewards. The thought of seeing Face and Spam tomorrow is a thread of delight in and of itself as well. We are camping out with more southbounders tonight, and we are again exchanging information that hikers from the opposite direction

can't get enough of. Nothing beats word of mouth when it comes to finding out the real information about the difficulty of the trail, the hospitality of towns and hostels, and the best deals for food along the way. The southbounders are happy to finally be out of Maine, just as we are excited to be so close to crossing that last state line. There are only three hundred miles between Katahdin and me right now, and I am feeling the end approach. I have given a lot of thought to when I should book my departure flight, and I have decided to book it tomorrow for July 26. That should give me a tidy amount of time to complete the hike and get to Logan International Airport in Boston.

Yikes just arrived at the shelter, so Sensei and I are in even better spirits. She told us about how she went down the wrong trail on Mount Adams and made camp alone and away from the AT. She made excellent time up the Wildcats and matched our pace so well that she arrived here just a few hours after we did. We all couldn't be happier; the shelter we are in is filled with triumph, celebration, and anticipation of the final stretch of this amazing trail that has brought so many incredible aspects into our lives that we didn't know we were looking for.

July 5

What a celebration. Yikes, Sensei, and I hiked eight miles of mosquito-infested downhill beauty to the White Mountains Lodge and Hostel, where Face and Spam would meet up with us. There is something delightful about discovering that a place is just as wonderful as its reputation. When we got to the hostel (right along the trail, so no hitchhiking necessary), we recognized the shoes, packs, and tents that belonged to our friends. I followed suit and unpacked everything so that the warm sunshine could dry everything from the last few days' worth of rain.

This hostel had comfortable beds, laundry facilities, breakfast and dinner, and Internet and even offered shuttle rides into nearby Gorham; everything a growing hiker needed. After we showered and changed, the three of us got a ride into town at lunchtime. We saw and enjoyed the Independence Day festival that was going on, and it looked like everyone in Gorham turned out to see it. There was live music, carnival rides, contests, and food and drinks everywhere. After we replenished our food supplies at the supermarket, we went back to the hostel, had a wonderful home-cooked lunch, and drank a few New Hampshire–brewed beers. Yesterday evening I booked my flight online from Boston to Albuquerque, and the very act was a little bit sad since it meant that the hike is almost over. My flight is set for July 27, just three weeks from today; only 297 miles of AT stands between us and Katahdin.

I have been sending postcards and e-mails to Mom and Andrew to let them know I'm OK, and I really ought to call them today before heading back out on the AT. I love Mom, but I just can't get excited about phone calls that are full of emotional distress and relentless guilt. She always makes an effort to make me feel useless, irresponsible, and selfish for doing this hike, but I feel none of it. The truth is I have never been more in tune with nature or myself and consequently have honestly never felt so alive. Whenever I talk about the benefits of this adventure, Mom likes to quickly change the subject. I don't know if she is jealous or disgusted by my stories, but I don't feel like I can share them with her like I can with Andrew or my friends. I am so thoroughly imbued with joy and peace of mind that I don't want a conversation with her to spoil it. Am I a bad son? Perhaps I am.

The last time I celebrated Independence Day was with my family in Dallas in 2008, so I was way overdue for a July Fourth parade. The last two years were spent working hard in Iraq, and there wasn't a single parade for any reason. There was much for me to celebrate in Gorham, including my first stateside Fourth of July in three years, completing the hike through the White Mountains, catching up to my hiking friends, and making it all the way to Maine's doorstep. We were all in excellent spirits, and we had every right to be. The only times that got me down were during my chats with Mom. She never understood my motivation to hike the AT and took it personally that I didn't want to spend all the time when I wasn't working with her. I told her one of the reasons why I worked in miserable Iraq for two years was so I could accomplish this trail; it was much more than just a way to pass the time until my semester began. I wasn't even sure that I was fully aware of what this hike meant to me.

July 6

Welcome to Maine. This morning I hiked ten miles to the Carlo Col Shelter from the campsite I shared with Yikes, Spam, Sensei, Face, and Magic Bag last night. We left the hostel yesterday late in the afternoon with more than a little bit of reluctance, but we were all motivated to advance into the final state. I was a little bit buzzed from the pregame bottle of pinot grigio I had before leaving the hostel, which made for a surprisingly good seven-mile hike. I slept soundly last night, and I woke up bright and chipper this morning at 4:30 a.m. Porridge was for breakfast, and I got hiking an hour later. No one else was awake, so I left silently. It was a slow ten miles but not difficult. The best part of my morning was finally seeing a bear. I had already given up on seeing any bears since I went through the Shenandoahs and most of New Hampshire without having seen any, even though almost everyone around saw one. It wasn't as if I was hiking with my eyes closed; I saw countless deer, thousands and thousands of birds, and every bit of trail magic that was on the trail. I had accepted that bears didn't want to be anywhere near me. This morning's bear heard me approaching before I saw it, and when I trained my eyes on it, the bear was moving away from me into the nearby cluster of trees. I didn't take my eyes off it, even to get my camera; I knew that I would only see it for a few seconds, so I stood silently and watched it run away from me. I quietly thanked the bear for letting me see it and continued along at a brisk pace.

For lunch, I made cheddar and broccoli rice with couscous wrapped in tortillas. It is only noon, but I feel like I have had a full day already. I love it when a day has so much more, and today has another ten miles to go. I needed to take a break so I could eat lunch and get more water; if it wasn't for these things, I could go on indefinitely. I have Mahoosuc Notch to tackle tomorrow, which is reputed to be the slowest section to hike through on the entire trail. I wanted to write about my bear sighting while I had some time to kill; I'm thrilled to have finally seen a bear with my own eyes.

After all those weeks and months of hearing all the hikers around me catching sight of bears, bear families, and being invited to have tea and crumpets with bear communities, I was psyched to finally see my own big bear lumbering away from me, while hiking before sunrise. Nonhikers might wonder why it was so important to see a bear, and I suppose I just wanted to see with my own eyes what these majestic creatures were like in the wild, even if just for the briefest of glimpses.

July 7

Yesterday was fourteen miles, and today was sixteen miles; both days were exhausting enough to feel like twenty-five miles or more. This morning I scrambled over Mahoosuc Notch; it took me about an hour to cover the hardest mile I have ever crossed, but it was actually quite fun. I scraped my knees and knocked my elbows, but I liked putting my climbing skills to the test. I'm certain that hiking the last couple of weeks with only one trekking pole has improved my balance and hiking technique. Immediately after Mahoosuc Notch was the sharp ascent of Mahoosuc Arm, which was, for me, an enjoyable climb. The peaks that followed were slow going, and their descents punished my knees, but my mind was on the blissful weather; I couldn't be anything but happy all day. Tonight's shelter is jam-packed with the four of us and two southbounders; I haven't seen Yikes since yesterday. The plan is to hike big miles the next few days; I hope the terrain is more accommodating than it has been lately. I only have enough food for two more days, so I need to stop eating so heartily and make it stretch out more, or hope I come across some trail magic during the next couple of days. I am happy with my hike today from 6:00 a.m. through 5:00 p.m., and the trail magic of root beer and cheese crackers kept up my energy. Coming across trail magic is like discovering a hundred-dollar bill you didn't know you had in your pocket; that feeling never loses its luster.

July 8

Today was an easy fourteen-mile hike from the Frye Notch Shelter to the disappointing little hamlet of Andover. I crossed the peak of Bald Pate Mountain yesterday, and it struck me as one of the absolute best points on the AT. The trail was entirely below tree line; I wasn't rewarded with any vistas after the climbs, but my spirit soared, all the same. Standing just 246.5 miles from Katahdin, I am having a tough time realizing the huge distance I have hiked in such a short space of time. As long as I keep my head about me and watch where I step, this experience will be a major triumph that I will dwell deeply on for years to come. Never have I had so many amazing experiences and so many remarkable people enter my life as I have had these last couple of months. It is nearly impossible to take all of it in.

I think often about Mom and what I can do to improve our interactions. I don't like always talking about negative things with her, especially when there are so many positively bright experiences I'd rather discuss. The group of us took a lunch break at the Hall Mountain Lean-to (shelters are called lean-tos here in Maine); Yikes caught up to us, which put a smile on everyone's face. We missed her collegiate sense of humor, which fit in so well with all of ours. Everyone needed to resupply in Andover, so we went off trail, hoping for a welcome town respite. Drinks and showers would brighten an already happy day.

The hostel we stayed at in tiny Andover was comfortable enough and gave us the opportunity to shower and do laundry, but the town itself was barely anything to speak of. There was only a small general store (not much bigger than the tiny stores I came across in Iraq, actually) and a restaurant that looked much better than it turned out to be. The fish and chips everyone ordered took over an hour to get to the table, and our meals were mysteriously cold and bland. It was, hands down, the worst town visit I would experience on the entire AT, and for the first time I rejoined the trail eager to put as much distance between the town and me as I could. Maybe that was Andover's mission, after all.

July 9

We hiked twenty-six miles today. The hiking began at 6:30 a.m., and none of us were tempted to stay another minute longer than we had to in Andover. This morning we were awakened by a thunderstorm and readied ourselves to be shuttled to the trailhead at 6:00 a.m. Any hopes for a hot breakfast were dashed, but we sufficed with packaged apple pastries and coffee to go. The trail welcomed us with open arms. The first half of the day was difficult; I kept myself occupied by singing out loud to myself and conversing with hikers I met along the way. I made three liters of water last the whole day; rationing water has become a skill. The last four hours of today's hike were alongside Spam, and we flew like eagles along the AT. We all agreed to spend the night in Rangeley, and that town was an unexpected joy. Spam, Sensei, and I hitchhiked away from the trail first, but we arrived last because of the deranged driver who picked us up. We told the tale of the demonic driver to Yikes and Face over pizza and beers when we caught up with them. Face was especially humored, as he imagined me in agony with my knees folded up to my chin for the whole ride, so he paid for the second pitcher of Maine-brewed beer to ease our moods. I like being around these people!

After the most dreadful hitch into town I hope I will ever have in my entire life, I was relieved to escape the cramped car driven by a very unsober woman and her copilot; they acted as if they forgot we were sandwiched in the backseat. It took the driver forty minutes to give us a ride that was nine miles into town, which was far more painful than we expected. The floor was covered in motor parts, and I had to sit with my legs bent up to my chest, which aggravated my weary knees. The three of us thanked our benefactors curtly and gave them some gas money when they asked us to. I don't think I had ever wanted to get out of a car more than I did then, and I doubt that Sensei and Spam felt much better. It was my guess that the woman and her passenger friend were extremely high, maybe even mentally deranged. They drove us around maniacally and made us wonder if we weren't trapped in a nightmare. For being from such a small town, they got lost easily, we agreed.

July 10

Today was a surprise zero. We all felt after the tremendous effort of the last few days, we deserved to take a zero in beautiful Rangeley. We had plenty of time before we needed to be finished with the hike, so we accepted the fact that we didn't need to rush; it's OK to relax and spend some time in the places that appeal to us along the trail. I know I felt like I deserved some relaxation, so we availed ourselves of the town's accommodation. At a cost of twenty bucks per head per night, the lakeside hotel we stayed at was perfect. This morning began with a delicious breakfast (spinach omelet and coffee), followed by a food resupply at the supermarket. On the way back to our hotel, Face and I stopped at a small vendor and purchased a couple of "lobstah" rolls for four dollars each. They were amazingly delicious; Maine's reputation for seafood is not exaggerated. When we got back to the hotel, we all jumped in boats on the lake and went paddling around like kids. We kept our beers concealed and had the time of our lives that sunny Maine afternoon. For dinner, Face, Yikes, and I went to a local bar and enjoyed more of Maine's delicious food offerings and beer while we listened to "Paradise by the Dashboard Light" (one of Face's favorite songs). We rejoined Sensei and Spam at the hotel room and fell asleep watching movies on TV. We agreed that this was the best zero we ever had, and it resupplied our energy for two more weeks of hiking. The return to normal life is almost upon us, which for me means going to college and working toward my master's degree in business management. It will be a change of pace, but one that my knees will appreciate!

July 11

Yesterday, I feel I have to reiterate, was the best zero ever. Excellent seafood, boating, drinking beers, relaxing, and drinking mudslides until midnight with the vacationers next door. I was a little hungover this morning, but I made it better by eating an eggs benedict with seafood and salmon on an onion bagel, which no hangover can defeat. We got a ride to the trailhead, which was, thankfully, without insanity.

We hiked together for ten miles today and decided to hike twenty-three or twenty-six miles tomorrow. I am going to bed soon (maybe around 9:00 p.m.) because those Rangeley beers need to be slept off. I actually want to hike big miles tomorrow over tough terrain. There are just 209 miles until Katahdin, which is baffling in its smallness. I am reminded each day how lucky I am to have become a part of this group; we hike well together, and we consistently entertain each other both off and on the trail. But I've had enough of these huge blackflies biting my arms and legs. It is time to get inside the tent and hope that sleep and good weather fills my night.

The weeks were good to us and brought us hikers together in so many ways. It didn't matter whether we measured the trail in miles, months, or mountains, we found it within ourselves to do more than we thought was reasonable, if not possible. The midday naps under trees and dips in streams became normal living for the first time, and I couldn't get enough. After my back got used to the weight and my legs became used to twenty-five-mile distances each day, I never wanted the hiking life to be over. Rather, most of me didn't: there was always a part of me that missed the creature comforts of home and my nonhiking friends. Even so, I'll always remember the summer of 2011.

July 13

(afternoon)
Yesterday was grueling. I started hiking at 5:30 a.m. and didn't stop until 9:00 p.m. I covered 26.5 miles in about fifteen and a half hours, and my feet and knees were screaming for rest. We were touched by some rain, but the thunder was comfortably distant so as to not bother us. Face, Spam, and I made it to the agreed-upon shelter last night, but Sensei and Yikes must have camped out at the campsite we passed three miles earlier. Today Face and I are talking about doing just eighteen miles, which, I must confess, makes my body rejoice. My knees are feeling the toll of hundreds of miles, and I am

looking forward to giving them the rest that they need. I woke up late today and started hiking at 8:30 a.m., but I covered the hardest miles of the day. It is a little overcast, but the temperature is pleasant. The last couple of days have been a series of difficult mountains, and Face and I aren't shy about expressing our gratitude that this hike has an end. I am still happy to be on it, but I welcome the academia of my next adventure. I look forward to putting on gleaming white cotton shirts in the mornings instead of sweat-stained synthetic shirts. My feet, never the prettiest pair in any given lineup, are particularly knobby these days. However, there are a few more days of Appalachia to be enjoyed, and so I will not mistake pain for misery. Even after all these weeks, I still have to remind myself to drink more water and take more breaks. Why am I so inclined to devour big miles? I'm sure there is room for insight there, but right now I am content with just leaning back against my pack and letting the sun play on my face.

(evening)
Today turned out to be a ten-mile hike instead of the planned eighteen because Face, Sensei, and I were just obliterated. A few hours rest turned into an overnight stay at this shelter, so we planned out the logistics of crossing the Kennebunk River. The river, so we are told, can't be easily forded; everyone we have talked to tells us to use the ferry, which crosses it a few times a day. We expect to make it to the river the day after tomorrow, so it isn't necessary to pour on the miles today if we don't have to. Spam pressed on because he needs to pick up his mail package on Saturday in Monson before the post office closes for the weekend. I am looking forward to an early sleep tonight since I didn't get to sleep last night until very late. The southbounders we have encountered told us the terrain ahead of us is easier than what we have been dealing with, which is sweet, sweet music to our ears. We plan to arrive in Monson on Saturday, so I am eating lots of food to lighten the pack (not to mention I am ravenous). I think I will continue reading my Richard Dawkins book; it is fascinating.

Although I find the author to be a bit abrasive toward those who don't agree with him, I happen to like everything he points out. Even Face is already in his sleeping bag, calling it a day. I don't blame him; we have accomplished more than we ever thought we were capable of.

July 14

Today was a pretty good day, thanks to the more enjoyable terrain and the comfortable weather. Who am I kidding, I know the real reasons I am so upbeat: (1) tonight I am sleeping in a wonderful cabin and full-sized bed after having had a shower and watching the sun set over the forest with Face, Sensei, and Yikes; (2) in the morning, we are having a huge breakfast of a dozen pancakes, sausage, eggs, juice, and coffee; (3) in three days we will be arriving in Monson, which is the last trail town before the fearsome-sounding Hundred-Mile Wilderness; (4) in just eight days (*eight days!*) I'll be summiting Katahdin with my friends; and (5) this evening I had about half a box of Franzia zinfandel wine with some day hikers and Magic Bag at the shelter just half a mile from here. Oh, and (6) the Fellowship caught up to us today, and I got to share some of Katmandu's box of Franzia wine this evening, which was'nt awesome but I enjoyed it all the same. I think of all the hikers I have met who are about to climb Katahdin and wonder if any of them are as excited about their accomplishment as I am. I wish Kevin could have been here this week; he could be absolutely anywhere on the trail. So many friends, and I miss them all.

July 15

Other than stubbing my left toe on a tree root last night (Franzia, perhaps?), I enjoyed a perfect stay at the cabin. It was luxurious to have a full-sized bed to stretch out under the covers; maybe some creature comforts are worth having. There is a waterfall near the cabins, and it sings to me like music. It also gently woke me up, before any of the sun's rays crested the horizon. I don't even want to think about the nights I won't have gentle waters to send me to sleep after this hike. Just as I hoped for, the full breakfast was more than enough to satisfy the most ravenous appetite. It took some time to polish off thirteen of the best pancakes I've had in my life, and the delicious coffee I followed them with was made even better with the waterfall view. These weren't just any pancakes; our host made them with apples, blueberries, and raspberries in patriotic colors. The four of us agreed patriotic pancakes are not to be skipped—too bad Spam didn't get to enjoy them.

We left the lodge at 9:30 a.m. and hiked furiously. Good thing, too; if we had been just five minutes later, we would have missed the Kennebec morning ferry and would have had to wait five hours at the riverbank to be spirited across in the afternoon. As soon as we made it happily to the other side, we found two huge coolers filled with sodas, candy, snacks, and Smartfood popcorn. The breakfast and trail magic was all I needed to power me for the next five and a half hours to the next shelter; I didn't touch my food supply. When everyone arrived at the same shelter, we agreed that nineteen miles was sufficient and bedded down for the night. Tomorrow we will hike the remaining twenty-two miles into Monson, which suits us just fine. I am expecting Monson to welcome us warmly based on everything southbounders have told me. Working hard and playing hard is a routine I have become accustomed to.

I lay in my sleeping bag last night mentally preparing myself for the coming months of missing long-distance hiking; they will hit me hard. I reminded myself that I will be in the throes of a different adventure: higher learning. It will be less visceral than this one, but no less meaningful, I hope.

July 17

Even with high expectations, Monson managed to exceed them. We hiked twenty-two miles yesterday. Face called Shaw's Hostel and the caretaker arranged to give us a ride four miles into town. Since the only food I had was two snack bars, my pack was light and my pace was speedy. I wasted no time taking my shower and getting laundry done, and then I drank a pitcher of water as I checked e-mail and let people know how far along the trail I was. I had the feeling that I was surprising everyone not just by my quick pace but by making it this far at all. I never hiked much before I stepped on the trail; in fact, I would describe my pre-AT self as outdoors incompetent. As it turns out, I harbored a secret passion that even I knew nothing about.

We walked together into town wearing loaner clothes while our loads of laundry were drying. I proudly sported pajama pants and a Batman T-shirt I dug out from the community box at the hostel. I feasted on Maine lobsters that cost the very low price of seven bucks each. I thought I would never eat lobster this good for so little ever again in my life, so I had two. Fortune was smiling on us in Monson, because not only were we in town for a festival that brought out all the town's residents, but so was the Fellowship. We found them drinking at a bar by the pond and listening to live music. We joined them, and it was the last great hiker reunion our groups would see. All twelve of us couldn't have had more fun if we tried, and there were even fireworks. It was like a second Fourth of July!

The next morning I was groggy from the late-night celebrations, but excited. I could still taste all the lobstah, steak cubes, beer, and Ben & Jerry's in a drunken aftertaste. I brushed my teeth, and our group got ready to meet the Hundred-Mile Wilderness head on. We bade farewell to the Fellowship and Magic Bag before we got a ride back out to the AT. Partying with friends was a great source of energy that we would need to get through the tough final stretch that was all that stood between us at Katahdin glory.

The times we needed to escape the trail to replenish our food and supplies, properly bathe ourselves, do laundry, and connect with our friends and families at home to let them know we were more alive than ever were as memorable as the trail itself. I never had a chance to spend much time in small-town USA before I hiked the AT, and I was taken by the culture and customs that inhabited these places. Monson would have been among the best of these Appalachian towns, even if I wasn't surrounded by friends about to finish one of the best adventures of our lives. We left that place filled with gratitude, food, and excitement for the last leg of the AT.

The Hundred-Mile Wilderness is the most remote section of the AT. Hikers are urged to pack enough food for a week before venturing into it because resupply is almost impossible—towns are nonexistent. Personally, I was challenged by the notion of the wilderness; I wanted to hike without a safety net. It turned out to be one of my favorite parts of the trail, and the temporary absence of civilization was refreshing.

July 18

I am in unbelievable spirits. Today will be a twenty-mile day, and I already hiked half of those miles. The weather is exactly what I want it to be, and it feels good to have begun the Hundred-Mile Wilderness. Yesterday was actually the easiest town to leave (besides Andover, of course) because we were eager to sink our teeth into the last section of the AT. The Monson Festival was incredible; I loved having all the seafood, ice cream, and beer I could find, but the next eighty-eight miles are calling my very soul. I have just five and a half days left of hiking, and my days of hitchhiking are over, for now. I have passed through my last trail town where I must do laundry publicly, explain why, if I claim to be a functioning member of society, my beard is so long and straggly, and resupply my food bag. I will miss hitchhiking; no doubt I'll pick up more hitchhikers in the future now that I have been one for these last few months. I'm glad that I am nearly finished, but I still love the trail. This part of Maine is more enjoyable than the rocky bogginess of the first section, so my elation is untouchable. I am allowing myself to think more and more about my after-trail life, such the coming visit from Andrew and his family to Albuquerque in October for the International Balloon Fiesta. This is the first time my brother and his family will visit my home, and I want to make sure they have a great trip.

July 19

The weather couldn't be better for hiking. We have been hiking distances that allow for decent lunch breaks, the terrain has been moderate to easy, and the weather has been such that it could make anyone believe in a happy God (almost). Last night I slept in my tent again because the shelters have been filled with day hikers and with southbounders who are understandably doing small miles (they are on their first week of hiking, after all). Since there are only four more camping nights left on the AT, I wouldn't mind if they were all rainy and soaking wet (although, truth be told, I'd prefer these clear skies where I can see for miles from every peak). I feel like I could deal with anything at this point. This morning there were a couple of mountain climbs, but they were relatively easy and topped out with gorgeous long views of Maine. I was surprised to run into Stretch and Zippers, who I last saw at the Bear's Den around Mother's Day. They had jumped ahead and had already summited Katahdin, but hooked back to get in some extra hiking in sections that they passed over. They also took some time to place trail magic along the AT, which was certain to brighten any hiker's day. At the top of White Cap Mountain I saw Katahdin for the first time from a distance and gasped. There it was: the finish line. Today will be a nineteen-mile hike, so tonight I will fall asleep just sixty miles away from that seminal peak. Now that the terrain has become easier and there is plenty of amazing scenery, I feel like I did during the last week of high school: not much work left and plenty of time to spend time with my friends before we go our separate ways.

July 20

Today was another mix of excellent weather and fun trekking. Even the battalions of bugs can't get me down from this cloud. Last night we all tented next to each other alongside a stream and fell asleep by the sweet music of the rushing brook. It was the first thing I heard when I stirred awake, and it filled me with solace and peace. These are some of the best days I have experienced on the AT, which is saying something. The trail took us right past a sandy beach by Jo-Mary Lake, and since I had made quick progress, I saw no reason why I shouldn't take a two-hour swimming break.

It had been ages since I relaxed on a beach, so I took advantage of what nature presented today. I didn't have a care in the world and embraced the simplicity since it wouldn't last forever. The others joined me for a swim when they caught up, and we thought we were in Eden. Face opted to put on some speed and hike twenty-nine miles today, but the rest of us just didn't feel the need to do big mileage anymore. I just feel like keeping a peaceful and easy pace through gentle nature and not worrying about getting in late to a camping spot, hiking past sunset, or making detours off the trail when I'll be off it soon enough. Spam and I are already discussing how to spend the two days I will have in Boston before I fly home. His family has invited me to stay at their house until I leave, and I am more than happy to do so. It will be a nice way to bid a temporary good-bye to my hiking career. I will need to register for college next week, not to mention plan where I can take Andrew and his family to eat and visit in Albuquerque. I am allowing myself to consider the demands of normal life.

July 21

Tree roots, rocks, and boulders dominate the trail today. This puts my pace at 2.5 miles per hour, which isn't difficult, but it is annoying. As I hike, I can feel myself caught between two worlds: the wild one that has defined me for the past few months and the daydream world that anticipates Boston sightseeing, reconnecting with my brother and his family, relaxing in my Albuquerque home, and pushing forward in my academic pursuits. I still can't wrap my head around the fact that I have just thirty miles until I have the top of Mount Katahdin under my feet. Today threatens to rain, but the light raindrops that land on the canopy of leaves don't reach me. I wish it was sunnier, but I admire the cloudy sky that is typical of Maine.

A couple of hours ago I missed one of the AT blazes, took a wrong turn, and forded a stream I wasn't supposed to; I spent an hour looking for signs of the AT (and hikers) that weren't there. I double-backed across the stream and saw the turn I was supposed to make and continued on my way, relieved to be set right. This reminded me to not become complacent; I'm not finished yet. I just cooked my last hot meal on the AT: cheese and broccoli rice in a spinach tortilla (my absolute favorite). There are so many lasts happening. I was feeling a little overwhelmed until I let the breeze linger on my face and the essence of leaves and bark fill my nostrils, and then everything calmed down and I knew that peace is inside me. Yikes and I are being bombarded by bugs tonight, but we are enjoying the company of all the southbounders that we are camping with. Lots of laughs, smiles, and encouragement flow both ways. We have made it ninety-seven miles through the Hundred-Mile Wilderness and look forward to an easy-paced day tomorrow. These are good days.

July 22
We left the shelter this morning after bidding the southbounders an encouraging farewell and then headed north. We hiked just three miles to Abol Bridge and sat at the gas station picnic tables we found there to drink a few congratulatory beers for making it through the Hundred-Mile Wilderness alive. The last 9.5 miles were unbelievably easy, which suited my drunken pace just fine. I made great time since the terrain was smooth and level, as if in my dreams. It occurs to me that tomorrow will be the last time I wake up to the sunrise at 5:00 a.m. for a while. I have just three things on my to-do list for tomorrow: (1) hike up Katahdin; (2) take a picture with that famous sign on the peak; and (3) hike down. After we have our fill of Katahdin, all of us are meeting up with Spam's family and Sensei's family to eat and reminisce together. I am bringing a bottle of red wine to uncork at the summit tomorrow, which will go perfectly with my Clif Bars and Snickers. We are all hungover and are getting ready to rest up for what promises to be a full day of greatness. I feel the exact same way I did when I was eight years old on Christmas Eve: sleepy, but wildly excited for the morning.

July 24

What a rush yesterday was. I left the campsite at 6:00 a.m.; my feet were eager for mountain climbing. I wrote a journal entry in the ranger station register to all my hiker friends that I met on the AT. I thought hard about everyone I missed and gave one last shout out to them; they were as much a part of my hike as the rocks and soil beneath my feet, the leaves and breezes around me, and the sun and clouds above me. I wasn't compelled to carry my entire pack to the peak when I didn't need it, so I left the ranger station with two liters of water, my remaining snacks, and a bottle of wine (with corkscrew of course; what am I, uncivilized?). The light load made me feel streamlined and agile, and the strict climb was no challenge to me or the others in my group. It took just two and a half hours to make the journey from the campsite to the famous sign at Baxter Peak that declares to all the "Northern Terminus of the Appalachian Trail."

Face, Yikes, and I were the first of our group to reach the summit. The sun was new in the sky; once we stopped moving, it became chilly, so I put on my jacket. Another thru-hiker called Breeze caught up to us after weeks of following us and reading the journal entries we left at the shelters on the trail. He was delighted to finally put faces to our names and the stories he had followed avidly. Breeze passed around his beers and champagne, and I passed around my bottle of nondescript red wine.

"Still, it's better than Franzia," Yikes made sure to remind me with a smile.

We relaxed, told stories, and soaked up the sunshine and crystal-clear panorama around us. No wonder this place was the stuff of legend: it was one of the most spectacular places I have ever seen in these United States. By the time Spam made it to the peak with his family, we were all nicely buzzed. Sensei announced loudly to everyone on the mountain peak that Spam had carried his heavy pack 2,200 miles from Springer Mountain in Georgia to this peak. The mountaintop congregation exploded in cheers and applause. Spam came up to us and shrugged off his heavy pack; it still had every item he used on the trail. This was something he told us about weeks ago; he was proud of himself for going against the ultralight flow.

After about five hours of relaxing at an altitude of 5,267 feet and feeling like gods and goddesses, we decided to head back down. This would be the final chapter for everyone else, but I had committed to returning to hike the southern part of the AT next year. The descents were difficult for the poorly equipped and well-manicured vacationers around us, but for us they were easy going, and we made short work of the downhill climb. At the bottom, we met up with Sensei's family, who were easy to recognize—they looked so much like him. They took us to a campground where we could shower and change into clean clothes.

Before sunset, we all met up at the Loose Moose restaurant where we filled up on exquisite food, loud storytelling, libations, and laughter. Victory embraced all of us, and we savored the moment, and I don't think I'm alone when I say that everyone at that table will remember that night fondly for the rest of their lives.

This morning, we slept until the unforgivable hour of 8:00 a.m. and then eagerly got together for breakfast with Sensei's and Spam's families. I had the Millennium Special, and we all signed the ceiling tile the restaurant had for triumphant hikers to sign their trail names. We examined the tile together and laughed as we recognized our friends' colorful signatures.

Sensei and his family got up first, and we all hugged and thanked each other. Spam's family offered to take Face and Yikes to the Bangor Airport, so we rode together for one last leg. After Spam and I bade our friends an emotional farewell at the airport, we continued on to Boston.

Spam's family made me feel welcome in their comfortable and cozy home. Although I thanked them profusely, I don't know if they understood the depth of my gratitude. It is a welcome change to not be covered in mosquitoes, but my legs feel guilty for not hiking miles anymore. They'll have to get used to it, because soon it will be time for my brain to start doing all the work. I have heard about people gaining weight after they finish a hike like this, so I mustn't overindulge at mealtimes anymore. I am skinnier than I have ever been, but I know that will change before long. I confess, I am a little worried about gaining unwanted weight, but I tend to think these days that challenges are just successes waiting to be earned. I think back to the first few days of the hike in Virginia, and I remember the agonizing foot pain and self-doubts about ever finishing: Could it really have been only three months ago? Am I ready to rejoin society and face people that won't understand why I hiked the AT? I'm not sure, but I have a feeling that after a bit of a rest I will want to get back out here and finish what I started.

The day I climbed up Katahdin was nothing short of magnificent. It was the toughest climb on the trail, but my friends and I moved along past the day hikers with a skilled quickness that made us look like we had been mountain climbing our whole lives. The trail was populated with amateurs who were crying from the pain and whining about the difficulty; they watched us with envy as we overtook them with silent grace. We had a simple, yet memorable few hours on the peak. We congratulated each other as we made it to the sign that marked the official north end of the AT, took individual and group pictures, drank wine, smoked cigarettes, and ate the rest of our trail snacks, as more and more hikers made it to the top. I was almost moved to tears by the spirituality of the mountain and what it meant that my friends and I were there. None of us had broken any limbs, gotten robbed, or lost our faith in the journey. I tried to soak up the events of the last several months and feel the reward that was the majestic panorama we admired. The sky was clear of all but a few fluffy clouds, and the sun greeted us like a happy friend. Years later, I still remember that day on Katahdin's peak with reverence, and it always makes me feel better, no matter how sad I might be.

Before I became Windscreen, I was satisfied with hiking only the northern two-thirds of the AT. Now that I had sunk my teeth into it and tasted the unique deliciousness of thru-hiking, the hunger increased. I had to get back home to get started with college, but I knew I would be back east and on the AT again to finish what I started. As much grief as I felt at finishing the hike, I was looking forward to returning home to friends and my own domain. I'd like to tell you that I am an untethered spirit, a leaf on the breeze of cosmic happenstance, but part of me is comforted by the sense of home. I love waking up in a comfortable bed, knowing that I can have coffee on the patio downstairs without intruding upon another soul. To exist and to do as I want without permission or concern of others is a rare delight.

I have to be a custodian to the satisfied homebody as well as the traveling pilgrim. Fortunately, I wouldn't have to wait very long before I could answer to Windscreen again and dust off my trekking poles for more adventure.

OFF THE TRAIL FOR THIRTEEN MONTHS

When I returned home to Albuquerque, I reunited with my old friends who were glad to see me alive and well. They commented on how much weight I had lost and how thick my legs were. Of course they wanted to know about my adventure over the last few months, but I had to take caution. As eager as my friends were, I quickly grasped that I was much more keen to talk about the AT than they were to keep hearing about it. The frustration stems from the same burden that worldly travelers have when they return home: family and friends, no matter how well-meaning they are, are unable to understand the personal importance that the Appalachian Trail held for me. Once the reunion had happened and I told my friends about a few of the cursory details of the hike, I could see in their eyes their interest waning and knew I should wrap it up. I'm not alone in this: the other hikers noticed the same thing. I, like them, could talk nonstop about the AT, but only with others who had hiked it. Maybe this is what Thomas Wolfe meant when he said "You can't go home again."

But I was home again, and I needed to make it work. The AT was in the past, and I needed to get my head in the present. Less than two weeks after I summited Katahdin, I took my first step toward my next summit: a master's degree in business management. With the exception of a few classes, the subject matter interested me more than it might have sounded, and I became a full-time student.

I visited my mother and brother in Texas and shared a few stories and pictures with them. They had their own lives going on, but it was nice to discuss a little about the trail with them, even though they didn't share the hiking spirit that posessed me. Talking about my future travels and someday completing the AT instead of staying in Albuquerque to find a nice, quiet, simple job was disconcerting for my mother, but she supported me more and more as she go to know who I had become. She realized that my dreams weren't just fantasies, and that I wasn't going just through a phase. She kept busy with her successful security alarm business in Dallas, and Andrew had more than enough on his plate with his job and his family. It seems that we each share a passion for staying busy and productive in our lives, no matter how differently we devote our efforts.

I focused on building up my upper body strength, and I took a few yoga classes to improve my flexibility, which had disappeared after months of moving up and down mountains like a pack mule. Months of rigorous hiking with thirty pounds on my back had taken a toll on my knees (I was thirty-five, after all). I found that I couldn't go on my morning jogs anymore without my knees complaining; I became fearful of my physical health, not to mention concerned about how I would stay in shape without doing cardio. After many recommendations from my brother and a few friends, I started taking glucosamine. I kept my cardio workouts to elliptical machines so that I could stay in shape with as little impact to my legs as possible. After a month, I noticed my knees were beginning to recover, and after two months I was able to run for a sustained hour like I could before the hike. I'm back, baby!

Once I got in the swing of things, and my body had mostly recovered from the AT, I adopted a comfortable routine of exercise and relentless studying. I was excited for the career prospects that might open up to me once I had earned my degree, and I wondered if I could finally steer into a more academic career, while simultaneously finding one that allowed me to travel around the world. The promise of new possibilities was a golden carrot that dangled in front of me and kept me motivated through each class, exam, and written essay.

Even though I was content on the course I was on, I never forgot that I wanted to hike the southern part of the AT, and it took a phone call from my dear friend JP for me to start making concrete plans.

JP and his girlfriend Francessca were halfway through their months-long tour of Europe, Africa, and Asia. I enjoyed seeing their pictures on Facebook and following their occasional updates, and for a while I had to live through them vicariously while I delved into my studies. In January of 2012, JP called me on Skype.

"Homan!" He greeted me with his educated Tunbridge Wells English accent.

"Japes, you magnificent bastard!" I replied. "How the hell are you?"

"I'm good, and so is Francessca. We're in Thessaloniki, Greece, and we're going to Turkey tomorrow. In a few months we'll get to India, and then Nepal after that."

"Damn, JP, you're having the time of your life. I'm envious. I sure wish I could join you in Nepal instead of having to write about business management and law."

"That's why I called—we want you to join us. We plan to stay in Nepal for a month and do some hiking in the Himalayas. Can you take a semester off and meet us there?"

"Really? That sounds incredible! The fall semester lasts from August to late October...what if I take a break from university then?"

"That would be splendid." JP agreed. "So we can plan to meet in Kathmandu the first week of August, say?"

"I don't see why not."

"Good. Let's put a pin in that and iron out the details soon...I am about to be cut off, but I wanted to discuss this with you instead of via e-mail."

"I'm glad you called. I'm excited. I'm going to see my friends JP and Franscessca. In Nepal!" It sounded fantastical when I heard the words out loud.

After we hung up, I began to put together a plan for the fall. I thought that wondered, if I took a semester off to spend a month in Nepal with my friends, what I would I do with the other two months once I returened stateside?. The answer was obvious. My southern AT hike began to come into focus. I realized that if I took three classes in the spring and two in the summer, I would have just one left to take in the winter after my semester off. I love having a timetable to work by, and it was exciting to plan Nepal and the AT in the same year. It was almost overwhelming, and I was pumped.

Months of academia passed before July came, and if I hadn't been kept so busy, I would have been driven insane by impatience. JP and I touched base from time to time so we could agree on what trail we would hike in the Himalayas, and we finalized our travel dates. Before I knew it the time had passed, and I was packing for Nepal.

I spent most of August hiking with my friends on the Annapurna Circuit in Nepal. It had been a couple years since I saw Japes and Francessca, and we had a blast partying in Kathmandu before catching a bus to Besisehar, the tiny hamlet where we began our hike. I was delighted to discover how peaceful, friendly, and generous the Nepalis were, and the countryside was spectacular. There weren't many people on the Annapurna Trail, so it felt more serene at that elevation than anywhere else I had ever been.

My weeks in Nepal passed much quicker than I would have preferred, and if I didn't have the AT coming up immediately, I would have been miserable about leaving. I said good-bye to JP and Francessca and thanked them for inviting me to share a part of their adventure. They wished me success for the rest of the AT, and I began looking ahead to the next adventure. I would miss my friends and thought about them heading toward Hong Kong, stopping at new and interesting places along the way.

I spent a week in Albuquerque between Nepal and the AT to pre-pare. I underwent the cleansing ritual that awaits all travelers: the long shower at exactly my favorite temperature, the loads of laundry, the reading of stacks of mail (why do so many banks want me to refi-nance my mortgage with them?), and, of course, planning dates and lunches with friends. Those five days in Albuquerque were a welcome respite, but I was eager to get back out onto the AT. Despite missing Nepal already, I was enthusiastic about seeing the AT again. The tem-peratures would be cooling down, and I couldn't wait to hike through forests of turning leaves.

Yikes lived in Virginia, and she messaged me that week to tell me that she wanted to hike with me for a couple of days. It seems that I wasn't the only one who missed the AT and wanted more. I looked forward to seeing her again; returning to the trail with a Katahdin friend was going to be fantastic. I grabbed my pack and trekking poles and flew to Virginia for the second time. I had never known such excitement as I had felt that year.

SOUTHBOUND FROM ROANOKE

August 23

(morning)

I am psyched! I woke up in my Albuquerque bed an hour before my 4:00 a.m. alarm, packed up the last of my things, looked around to make sure the house was copacetic, and locked the door. My dear friend and neighbor Dave offered to take me to the airport in exchange for coffee and bagels at Einstein Bros, which I happily accepted. Before I left the house, Dave's wife, Kathy, gave me a strong hug. I knew she was as excited as me, just a little more worried about me returning to spend months in the wilderness again. After a series of flights from Albuquerque to Chicago, and Charlotte, I arrived in Roanoke.

When I walked out past security I immediately found Yikes waiting for me. I quietly walked up to her and gave her a hug, surprising her from her smart phone.

"Windscreen!"

"Yikes!"

We must have sounded strange to anyone observing, but we gave up those kinds of concerns a long time ago.

We excitedly caught up and discussed how long Yikes would be able to hike with me. She wanted to hear about Nepal, and I wanted to hear about her adventures, too. We decided we needed to find some good beer to fuel our second AT adventure.

I checked into the same Best Western I stayed at before my Appalachian hike last year. It is surreal to see Yikes and be in this part of the country again, about to step back onto the trail I have been obsessed with since I left Boston last July. The two of us ambled around downtown Roanoke and found a Thai restaurant whose food tasted as good as it looked. Then we hung out at the TGI Fridays next to our hotel and had drinks while we reminisced about the AT. We caught up on each other's events of the past thirteen months and talked about our goals for the future.

This morning I woke up at 7:00 a.m. and saw that the sky was sunny, a good omen for a good hike. Twelve miles seemed like a good first day, so we agreed to meet on the top of Dragon's Tooth. I'm enjoying every bit of the trail before the aches and blisters kick in.

On the way to Virginia, I finished reading Into the Wild, *a story that had me captivated to the point where I almost missed a connecting flight in Dallas. Jon Krakauer relates the ambitions and adventures of Christopher McCandless, as he shrugs off his parents' expectations after college graduation. He ventures away from the cities, the social machine, and the entrapment of money. I won't give away the entire story because I think everyone would benefit from reading the book for him- or herself (or at least watching the movie version, superbly directed by Sean Penn and accompanied by Eddie Vedder's musical contribution). The story gave me much to think about as I wrestled with the opposing forces of domestic and "responsible" living versus debt-free, untethered, globe-trotting freedom, especially as I was in the process of weighing my life compared to one like JP's. I could identify with Chris McCandless to the point that it bothered me, especially his readiness to journey alone if he had to. The story made me consider my own life and where it was headed. I was nervous but ready to reunite with the trail. Yikes stopped at the Walmart on the way to the AT to let me stock up on a week's supply of food and then drove me to the trailhead. It was the exact place where I started my AT hike on April 15, the previous year, and it was a surreal, welcome sight. While I hiked, Yikes drove south to a hiker hostel near the trail and got a ride back north to meet me at Dragon's Tooth. I gave her some gas money, and we both got started on our respective journeys.*

(evening)

I can be so stupid sometimes. The day started out wonderfully; Yikes dropped me off at Route 311 where it crosses the AT, at the spot where I started hiking last year. This time I had the equipment and the mind-set of a pro. After too many beers, I should have re-plenished my fluids better than I did; I am paying for it now. I be-came dehydrated after hiking 8.5 miles to Dragon's Tooth, before I even started making the strenuous climb. I was slow, weak, and depleted of any energy; the climb up the rocky mountainside was an unexpected challenge, which I had only myself to blame for. After I ascended Dragon's Tooth, I found Yikes waiting for me at the top. I gratefully drank half of her water since I was parched; it was stupid of me for getting so dehydrated. She didn't mind, since she had been hydrating herself during her drive south while I was hiking. I was absolutely wiped by the time we got to the shelter, and I cursed myself for being so foolish. She hiked much faster and easier than I did; I was sluggish due to sheer exhaustion. I feel better now that I've had four liters of water and a big dinner of cheese and broccoli rice (I still love this particular flavor, even after all these months). Despite my agony, I am glad to be outside and enjoying a bugless night under the stars. The AT has welcomed me back into her arms.

I began this hike with all the equipment that would get me by. The begin-ning of the first hike was plagued by doubts about whether or not I was using the right gear (not too mention too-tight shoes and too heavy a load on my back); this time I hit the trail confidently, perhaps too confidently. The Merrill Moabs that I wore most of the trail last year were good enough to start this trek with (and I wear them for every hike to this day). My tent, a Big Agnes Fly Creek UL 2, was one of the only pieces of gear that I had from the start that I saw no need to replace, as were my Z-lite therm-a-rest sleeping pad and Vargo Triad stove (sans windscreen, of course). I had a brand new pair of trekking poles, and my trusty camera and Kindle, too. I thought myself bulletproof, even

to the point that I could hike ten miles effortlessly after a night of drinking with
Yikes without taking time to replenish my fluids. I promised myself I wouldn't
let myself get stupidly dehydrated again. What am I, new?

August 24

Eighteen years ago, the eighteen-year-old who would one day call himself Windscreen started US Air Force basic training. I couldn't possibly have guessed back in 1994 how my life would have led me to hike this crazy trail. It occurs to me that despite my well-planned ideas, I honestly can't know for certain where I will be eighteen years from this moment either. I started off today thinking I'd hike twenty-eight miles, but I decided at lunchtime that twenty-two would be enough. Then the blisters on my feet decided that sixteen miles was my limit and I should stop. I guess I'll have to work for a few days to get my trail feet back instead of jumping right into huge miles like I thought I might. Nepal was great for strengthening my endurance, but hiking in Virginia's heat was something I could only get used to in Virginia.

This section of the trail is experiencing a drought that makes water sources unreliable, so I am watching my water consumption as well as refilling wherever I am lucky to find replenishment. The water here is incredibly dirty; I have to filter it through my bandanna before I drink it. I can see the particles floating in it. Here's hoping I don't get sick!

I hope I can hike twenty-one miles tomorrow; I feel energetic and strong enough, but my feet have different plans. The weather was stunning again today, so I don't have to contend with rain-drenched socks. I hiked along the Audie Murphy Trail this afternoon and spent some time at the memorial as well. After working for two years alongside the army, I knew how revered this man was, and I took the time to pay my respects. Daylight ends sooner than I was expecting, but that just means I'll have to get used to night hiking again. I finished reading *Abraham Lincoln: Vampire Hunter* and left it as a gift at one of the shelters I passed. I love that feeling where I can start a new book; I have so many to choose from.

I can't remember many times in my life where I was as thirsty as I was those first few days back on the trail. I hadn't considered how much I would sweat in the Virginia summer and had only brought two liters with me. I also thought that the water spots in The AT Guide *were guaranteed (like they were heading north), but the drought had dried many of them up, so I was unable to refill along the way. I drank the filthiest water I've ever had, but I never got sick from it. I'm not sure if it's because I have a strong constitution or if the water was free of contaminants. I'm just grateful everything worked out as well as it did. Welcome back to the AT!*

August 25

Foster's lager at noon today. Fresh water and Girl Scout cookies were waiting for me at the side of the AT in coolers labeled "For Appalachian Trail hikers." Oh, trail magic, how I love you! The bottled water was more than welcome after the dirty water from yesterday. I came across two Virginia gents who were enjoying an afternoon in the woods with some beers and invited me to have a couple with them. Because she was hiking so fast, Yikes missed the first couple of trail angels, but we met up after our twenty-one-mile day of hiking. This time we both felt great. My blisters are under control, my legs are strong, my body aches (but only a little bit), and I feel myself improving day by day. Tomorrow we will hike twenty-three miles into Pearisburg, so it will be a long, rewarding day. I am glad to be back here in the wilderness; it is my place to be.

August 26

We started our twenty-four miles from Bailey Gap before sunrise and finished in Pearisburg just before 5:00 p.m. It was a long hike that bore down on my knees, reminding me of the long and harsh descent down Mount Adams last year. But I was motivated to get to my first town as a southbound hiker on the AT. The Chinese buffet we went to was mediocre, but plentiful. That combination is exquisite to hungry hikers. We finally ate ice cream and drank beer together for the first time since Abol Bridge last year. I have missed towns like Pearisburg that offer food aplenty, cheap hotels, and big supermarkets, all within walking distance of each other. This motel reminds me a lot of the one that Face Jacket and I stayed at when we stopped through Daleville my first week as a northbound hiker. *Sherlock Holmes* is on TV, and I can feel myself being lulled to sleep as I struggle to finish this journal entry. It has been a long time since a shower has meant so much to my mind, soul, and body—it is thoroughly exuberant. Tomorrow is my last day to hike with Yikes since she is parked at the Woods Hole Hiker Hostel; she has her life to go back to as I continue along with the AT. The trail is less populated this time of year and in this direction, so I am preparing myself to be alone more often than when I was going north. I must take care to hike safely and not suffer any breaks or illnesses. I suppose I could say that I take care against that sort of thing all the time, but here it matters even more.

August 27

What a perfect day. After Yikes and I ate breakfast at Dairy Queen, I picked up some denatured alcohol from the nearby hardware store and resupplied at Food Lion. We got back on the trail and began our hike to Woods Hole. Ten miles never felt so good. The sharp ascent out of Pearisburg was exhilarating and burned away the bloated feeling I had from drinking too much water before I left town. Today's hike was the easiest stretch I have experienced on the AT, and the sensational weather didn't hurt either. We hiked well together and chatted about science, politics, religion, and family. The day flew by, and we arrived at gorgeous Woods Hole at 3:00 p.m. All of the praise that I saw heaped upon this resort was justified; the meals they serve are as delicious as they are healthy. I'm anticipating missing Yikes already: the next few days, I'll be hiking south through Virginia by myself, which will make it different than my northbound hike, but I'm certain it will still be a phenomenal journey. I flipped through the trail journals that are piled up at this place; I enjoyed reading the entries of several northbound friends when they stayed here a year and a half ago. I miss all of those guys, but now they're getting on with their own lives and I'm hiking the rest of the trail before I finish my last semester of graduate school. After I finish my degree, I'll look for a job as a contractor overseas, probably in Afghanistan or Saudi Arabia. With that in mind, I will focus on the AT and make the most of the last long-distance hike I will get the chance to do for a few years.

It became apparent almost immediately that hiking south would be quite different than hiking north. Not only were there fewer hikers, but the weather would soon cool down, and I was looking forward to seeing the foliage turn colors in autumn. It was fun to meet as many hikers as I did last year, but the southern hike would be more solitary, maybe even more spiritual. It would be a different side of the same trail, and I was keen to experience it.

Being on better terms with my mother was a big improvement to my hike as well. Our conversations were infrequent, but positive, so I was able to make miles without added emotional weight. I chatted with Andrew when I could, but I usually just texted him that I was making progress whenever I had a good cell phone signal. Riverguide wasn't with me this time, so I was glad that I didn't have any problems that I needed to talk out, like I did in Duncannon last year. It is difficult to overstate how valuable family support is during ventures like this one.

August 28
The Woods Hole rooster woke me up at 7:30 a.m., and I immediately packed my stuff and got ready for the hike. Breakfast was at 8:30 a.m.; I ate a generous serving of broccoli, eggs, and sorghum pancakes. I thanked the kind hosts before I departed at 9:45 a.m. and felt like a champion for the rest of the day. I planned to hike fifteen miles, but I did twenty instead. Tomorrow will be a twelve-mile day because I need to resupply at Bastian. I came across two northbounders, but they weren't that chatty, so we kept going our respective ways. I'm crashing at Jenny Knob tonight with a northbounder who calls himself Sailboat. He is a South African whose family has been living on a boat for the last ten years, so he makes for an interesting conversationalist. He told me that I should stay at the Dojo tomorrow in

Bastian, and the host is an angel for AT hikers, so I think I will follow his advice. There has been such little water on the trail; it has been a delicate matter to keep myself adequately hydrated between distant and scarce water sources. That being said, water consumption is currently my only stressor, so I am making sure to enjoy the stunning world around me. It is just as good to finally be out here hiking again as it has been in my dreams. I have missed this trail, and we are getting along again famously.

August 29

What an easy day; twelve miles never flew so quickly. I left the shelter at 7:00 a.m. and arrived at the road to Bastian at 10:45 a.m. I had excellent cell phone reception, so I called Tru Brit, the host of the Dojo, who offered to pick me up at the trailhead. His comfortable place is near an all-you-can-eat pizza bar as well as a store where I can get all the food to last me until I get to Atkins. I found myself missing my hiking buddies, so I called up Sensei and Face to let them know where I was and how different it was hiking south from hiking north. I plan to hike twenty-two miles tomorrow and the day after, so I am enjoying watching *Seven Years in Tibet* on The Dojo's big screen. The movie captured the Himalayan majesty that I had just experienced in Nepal, so I was especially taken with the film. How can it be possible to love being in one place, while simultaneously desperately wish to be someplace else?

It seems like there are more towns along the trail this far south than there were heading north from Roanoke, so I might not have to carry as much food on the trail as last year. I stocked up on food for the next two days and will press on early tomorrow morning.

The Dojo and my host, Tru Brit, were pleasant. I was surprised by my host's political leanings, and I listened with disguised amusement as he told me about the Obama conspiracy to allow Muslims to take over the nation. He watched Fox News religiously and preached the decline of the American economy. I wasn't comfortable disagreeing with someone who let me spend the night under his roof, so I just listened and ignored the temptation to express my opinions. I actually enjoy hearing people's opinions; they force me to reassess my own and consider other points of view.

August 30

I ate well yesterday and again this morning before I headed out. Although Tru Brit and I hold different political opinions, I was glad to have met him and visited the Dojo. I hiked my planned twenty-two miles to the Chestnut Knob Shelter, which is situated in solitude on a peak in between a tough climb and an imposing descent. The altitude here is 4,409 feet, which is pretty high for Virginia. I look forward to visiting Atkins tomorrow so I can get some more iodine tablets. My legs are pretty strong now, but I still enjoy these town breaks. I rarely see other hikers; it isn't nearly as populated hiking in this direction, especially at this time of year, as it was hiking north. I miss the crowds, but I also enjoy the silence; it gives the trail a quiet peace that makes me feel as if I am the only hiker in existence. I was elated to come across some water at a trail magic spot halfway through my hike today, and it couldn't have come at a better time. Every water source that *The A.T. Guide* specifies is dry; the drought is that intense. I probably wouldn't make so many town stops if the AT was wetter, but the truth is I don't mind getting to see more of small-town America. It is a bit weird to be hiking the opposite direction to what I hiked last year, but only when I think about it.

August 31

I slept in solitude at the Chestnut Knob Shelter and departed just before sunrise at 6:30 a.m. The night was chilly, but I kept warm in my trusty sleeping bag. Wet fields led to big climbs and hard descents, but I hiked twenty-three miles like a trooper. My concerns about water were made easier by drinking only when I needed to, and the occasional trail magic along the way helped enormously. I gave thanks to a kind old woman who welcomed me onto her porch and invited me to drink my fill of ice-cold, crystal-clear water. She couldn't believe how much I drank; I must have been parched. I conveyed to her how supremely thankful I was for what she thought was a small gesture. I know she didn't understand how she rescued me from an afternoon of sucking air through a dried-up throat into dusty lungs. I sat in one of her rocking chairs as I felt my innards soaking up every droplet, singing praises to the charitable lady who extended a hand to a stranger she would certainly never see again. She was as happy to help me as I was to accept her help, and we both cherished the shared moment of humanity. That thirty-minute break powered me up and allowed me to quickly eat up the next eleven miles to the small town of Atkins. I was exhausted, but happy to be there. I showered off the layer of dusty trail and devoured a Hiker Burger—the jewel of a restaurant called the Barn. I never had a burger made from an entire pound of beef before, but I devoured it with enthusiasm. I'm planning to hike eleven miles tomorrow; even if I don't come across much water, I can still get some miles under my belt.

September 1

Today was Saturday, but it was, as Lionel Ritchie sings, easy as Sunday morning. I woke up bright and cheerful at 8:00 a.m., ate a satisfying breakfast at the Barn, chugged two whole bottles of Gatorade, and departed Atkins at 11:00 a.m. It took just four hours to hike those eleven miles to the Mount Rogers Visitors Center, where I took the opportunity to order a spinach, tomato, and feta-cheese pizza. I sat on the outdoor steps and lazily ate my delivered pizza in the bright sunshine, since the next shelter was only a quarter mile down the trail. Before I left the visitors center, I left a two-liter bottle of Pepsi because I was thankful to the employees for letting me loiter there, even if it was after hours. After I stuffed my face and drank aplenty, I hiked the arduous quarter mile to the Partnership Shelter, which was magnificent. It had been built recently and was big enough to sleep twenty hikers; it was nestled snugly in the woods, under the treetops and starry sky. Once again, I am alone tonight (I have never seen so few hikers on the trail). I think I will focus on doing bigger miles since there isn't much else to do. It is expected to rain tonight, thanks to Hurricane Ivan, so I am wrapped up snugly in my sleeping bag, tucked in at the back of the shelter. I finished reading *China in the 21st Century*, so tonight I started reading *From Socrates to Sartre*, which Johnny Appleseed recommended to me last year. I projected my hiking tempo over the remainder of the trail, and even if I take my time the way I have been, I will get to Springer Mountain in less than five and a half weeks. That time will fly, so I'll make sure to keep my eyes on the trail and not be too concerned with searching for a job in the new year—easier said than done.

September 2
I had an excellent time hiking thirty miles to Wise Shelter today. If I do about twenty-four miles tomorrow, I'll have just eight or nine miles to hike into lovely Damascus on Tuesday. My feet are feeling pretty raw, but overall I feel like a thoroughbred. During the first break I took today, I met two section hikers called Jordan and Andrew. We chatted nonstop for the hour and a half I stayed there, all about the ups and downs of the trail. I love how everyone is breathtaken by so much beauty. Is it because the trail is full of optimists, or does hiking bring out the best in us? Maybe it's both.

My second break of the day was at the Orchard Shelter, where I stopped and chatted with several section hikers about the trail; you can mine an endless number of conversations from this single topic. I arrived at this shelter just after the last rays of twilight; it is full, and we are packed close like sardines. I hope no one snores tonight, because I am exhausted. It is a welcome change to be around all these Labor Day weekend hikers. I am catching up to the thru-hikers ahead of me; I can tell by their journal entries at the shelters. It will make me happy to geek out about the AT the way only thru-hikers can. There have been, thankfully, more water sources along the trail; I feel healthier and more nourished than I have all week. I'm also glad that it hasn't rained much during this hike; I still remember how having wet socks for days felt, and I'm not eager to relive that sensation again anytime soon. The autumn weather appears to be approaching, so I can't wait to see the leaves turn and temperatures drop.

September 3

Happy Labor Day. There are hundreds of section, weekend, and day hikers on the AT, and I love the interesting company. I'm staying at the Saunders Shelter tonight, and it looks like it will be just me here. The rain is coming down hard, so I am grateful for the shelter. I can't stop staring at the flower colors around me; the forest colors pop almost extradimensionally. I hiked for about forty minutes through the refreshing shower before I arrived here; my socks are soaked, but I don't mind. Tomorrow I will hike into Damascus, which is a town full of excellent hosts and steeped in hiker admiration. Face Jacket was the first to tell me about this town during my first week hiking the AT, and I can't wait to see it. I'm only eight or nine miles away, so tomorrow will be a pleasant jaunt toward good food, Internet, laundry, and resupply. Yikes is absolutely right; one of the best parts of hiking the AT is the town visits. I took a break for an hour at the Lost Mountain Shelter 6.5 miles back, and the long respite worked wonders on my feet and legs. Frequent breaks are good for my body, and they allow me to push harder than I otherwise might. I ought to take more breaks, but I am always so eager to keep moving forward. Maybe I'll have this hiking gig figured out by the time I get to Springer.

A friend of mine I met in Iraq, Michaela, is stationed with the army in Georgia and wants to join me on the last part of the hike. I'm concerned that either I will hike too fast for her, or she will slow me down so much it will affect my enjoyment of the hike. I have considered asking her to meet me on the last day, but she wants to hike two or three days with me. I know the army hikes that she loved so much are nothing like sunup-to-sundown treks on the trail. She thinks she knows what to expect, but I don't think she does. I have to think of a way to politely tell her how strenuous AT hiking is and that she shouldn't underestimate it.

As of today I have just 474 miles left to hike; that number shrinks so fast, much faster than I'd like it to.

The change in seasons gave me a whole new experience on the trail; wholly different from the northbound venture, but not at all unpleasant. I started this hike at the end of summer, and I was glad that the hottest days were behind me. Autumn trees colored my hike that year in the best way, and I couldn't get enough of that fall smell. The northbound hike had been a nonstop party, and I was never far away from friends on the trail. This year I felt alone, but never lonely.

Oh, there were plenty of people on the trail, of course. The excellent weather and turning leaves brought out everyone who was near enough and eager to hike; there were day hikers, small-section hikers, or adventure groups out for the week. I rarely encountered other hikers who were taking on hundreds of miles, but over time I heard about them on the trail. As I came into my stride, I started meeting these southbounders. These guys were movers. Some needed to finish by a certain date, and others just wanted to get the hike over as fast as they could. I was soaking it up and wasn't interested in finishing the trail anytime soon. Every Appalachian day was my idea of heaven. Never in my life had all been as right with the world as it was on the trail. I had no financial problems and didn't need to start job hunting for another three months. I had no time crunch, since the next deadline I had was my friend John Manifold's November wedding in Phoenix. I felt like I had all the time in the world to enjoy every single waterfall, vista, mountain, and stream that I passed along the way.

I especially missed the friends I had made on the trail the year before. Most of them were in college or working at their jobs, but a few of them had gone on to hike the Pacific Crest Trail (PCT) on the other side of the country. I felt like I was more solitary than ever, but I realized that it would be over before I knew it. This world of nature, exercise, fresh air, and nights spent under the stars became even more a part of me than it did during the first hike.

September 4

I had an agreeable hike into Damascus today. It was a delight to see all the open stores and restaurants that were competing for my attention;

this has been the best town I have hiked southbound through. I ate a breakfast wrap just minutes after arriving and washed it down with a blueberry milkshake that reminded me of the ones I drank last year in the Shenandoahs. I decided to check out the Hikers Inn, and I am glad that I did. For thirty dollars I will have my own bed in the bunkhouse (by myself, since there aren't that many hikers these days), laundry services (cleaning and folding and all), and all the Internet I could want. I got a haircut, looked around town, and picked up a package from Sensei: Superman socks. There was even a little cape on the back of each sock. I was beside myself with laughter, and I promised to wear them the day I climb Springer. I put a yummy calzone in my belly and chased it with a few beers. Even in the drizzle, this town is picturesque; I like Damascus.

The southern nine hundred miles went quickly and easily, especially compared to hiking in New Hampshire and Maine. The farther south I went, the easier the trail was. My legs were at their best, and I loved every mile of it. Damascus was full of character, even in the constant rain. I was almost out of Virginia, which was a bittersweet accomplishment. I began both AT adventures in this state, so it would always be special to me.

September 5

It was difficult to leave the Hikers Inn this morning, but I managed it. It began pouring at 6:00 a.m., and I got ready to go so that by the time breakfast was available at 7:00 a.m. I wouldn't waste any time. I was on the AT by 9:00 a.m. and pressed through the rain. I was drenched in no time, but the omelet inside me filled me with bliss. I am happy to have passed through Damascus and am eager to see what lies ahead. When I sloshed up to that first shelter, I considered doing just ten miles. After all, I have plenty of time, so why rush? After an hour, the clouds broke to reveal the brightest sunshine, so I decided to hike in it. I hiked eight more miles to Double Springs Shelter and met Stray Dog, who I have been following for weeks in the trail journals. We chatted for a while and discovered we share similar outlooks on politics, religious beliefs, and economics. I'm glad I hiked eighteen miles today, because I can be flexible with the miles I put down tomorrow. I like having the freedom to go big or take it easy. I am beginning to realize how much I love hiking; it occurred to me today that I seriously need to start planning my work tempo around these long-distance hikes. I'm not sure how long it will be before I can afford to hike the PCT, but I hope to do it by 2016. That will mark a decade from when I first learned about the AT in Bill Bryson's *A Walk in the Woods*, the book that started Windscreen's hiking career.

The stops into town were great because I could satisfy my need to talk to people, even if we knew we would never see each other again. The outdoor-supplies stores usually were staffed with helpful people who could tell me what to expect in the miles ahead and what towns to avoid or take time to see. One of the most popular topics of conversation was where to eat. I discovered that hiking the AT was one of the best ways to experience small-town America. What the towns along the trail lacked in worldliness, they more than made up for with unique personality and enthusiasm for the hikers who passed through. I couldn't believe how good American pizzas could taste, how big and juicy hamburgers were, how satisfying blueberry milkshakes could be, or how tasty fresh Maine lobster was until I experienced AT towns.

September 9

With all the rain, mileage planning, and conversing with Stray Dog yesterday, I forgot to mention that I crossed out of Virginia and into Tennessee. I love passing state border signs. They aren't as spectacular as the state border signs that adorn interstate highways, but it's still a big deal when I pass them. Now that I have 424 miles left, I am concerned with figuring out when to book my return flight and how much time to allow myself to complete the hike. Last year I had a blast with Spam's family and spent some days checking out Boston's museums, restaurants, parks, colleges, breweries, and theaters. This year, it looks like I will be finishing unceremoniously and making my way to Atlanta on my own; I'd better start looking for couch-surfing hosts there now. Today I slept until 7:00 a.m. since the heavy rain was soothing and I didn't feel like hiking in the rain again. After an easy breakfast and an interesting discussion about Occupy Wall Street with Stray Dog, I decided to place my bet on the rain letting up and took off from the shelter at about 9:00 a.m. I ended up winning the gamble and managed to keep everything but my feet dry. I pushed on for 25.5 miles. I'm getting close to Kincora, home of the famous Bob Peoples; Bob is one of the heroes of the hiking community, not to mention of of the most interesting men in the world. Not only has Bob thru-hiked the AT and the Camino de Santiago, he is a tireless trail steward and he maintians one of the best hiker hostels in existence. No doubt he will be a fascinating person to listen to, and right now I wouldn't mind a chance to get dry and warm again.

September 7

The way it looks, I just might have this hike in the bag by October 5. This suits me just fine, since that gives me a couple of weeks before I need to get to Phoenix for John's wedding. I'm still mindful about watching each step; it wouldn't do well for the best man to sport a broken leg. Although I am taking care to not be reckless, I am moving effortlessly with the kind of speed that is usually reserved for superheroes. Today was an excellent series of ups and downs all the way to Kincora and met Bob Peoples. He is a wonderful man with the same spirit of adventure that I have. The man is in ridiculously good shape for being in his mid-60's, and his life is built of dreams as big as mine. I met two northbound hikers who started in Springer, and we all picked each other's brains about the AT. They spoke with unbridled enthusiasm about the Smoky Mountains, and I was sure to tell them about all my favorite parts as well. Bob let me do laundry and was happy to shuttle Stray Dog and me to a supermarket to stock up on food. During the drive, Bob told me about his treks along the AT and PCT as well as the Camino Santiago in Europe. I never seriously thought about doing it before today, but now it is on my radar, just like the PCT. I am never going to get tired of chatting with people like these in places like this and going on treks like this.

Is this enlightenment? Can it be that this AT gig went from a casual trip to a paradigm-shift-inspiring journey? It wasn't expected, but I like it. I'm starting to think that the AT isn't big enough to contain the adventures that it inspires.

September 8

Last night was great. Bob, Stray Dog, and I shared a long, sober, thought-inducing conversation that traipsed through the past and invited the future as we lingered joyfully in the present. It turns out that Bob was in the air force, so we exchanged flight-line tales into the wee hours this morning. We shared a few laughs about the trials and tribulations of aircraft maintenance until we were both too tired to keep our eyes open. It fascinated me to hear about another generation's air force experiences on the same C-130s that I worked on fifteen years ago. Today, I woke up at 7:00 a.m., shaved, and cleaned up before heading into the great outdoors. I leisurely hiked fifteen miles today through the beautiful weather and refreshing streams. There wasn't a single raindrop until I was five miles away from Mountaineer Shelter, where I am spending the night. I am feeling accomplished as I always do when I cross into a new century of miles. Now that I am just 398 miles from the end, I feel like I should take stock of each and every ray of sunlight, breath of wind, and turn of leaf. Maybe I can even appreciate the rain.

The weather got cooler and the surroundings became even more beautiful when September arrived. As I entered the Smoky Mountains, the copper and red leaves commanded my rapt attention. The combined hikes of Nepal and the AT were a double-punch of reality for me, instead of an escape from reality. Unlike everyone else, I viewed the years I have to work as the escape from reality, preferring to think of traveling adventures as my real world. Maybe I'll be lucky one day and have a job that doesn't pull me from my reality. The only people who seemed to agree with my perspective were JP and Francessca (Jesus, I missed them).

September 9

Last night was freezing. Tonight will be too, especially since I will be staying at the highest shelter on the AT. The Roan High Knob Shelter sits at 6,285 feet and will be a welcome reward after my twenty-five-mile hike today. Not that I need a reward; today was probably the most scenic day along the AT I can think of this year. The weather was clear enough for me to see for miles around from the mountain peaks. The Hump Mountains were as dramatic as their name suggests, and Roan Mountain was especially satisfying. I'm considering doing twenty-nine miles tomorrow; it always depends on the subtleties of the trail, and I must keep myself flexible for unexpected challenges. I know it is going to be difficult to get out of my sleeping bag in the morning, so I am mentally preparing myself for a freezing start to the day. I have a feeling Stray Dog is pretty far behind me by now, and I have only seen two other thru-hikers going in my direction. I passed one today, and one passed me. Very few southbound thru-hikers are interested in hiking together, unlike northbounders who were more than happy to stick together.

Tonight I am 373 miles from the end, which means I'll need to book my flight next time I sit at a computer.

September 10

Damn, my feet are beat! Twenty-nine miles certainly feel like it. I am 344 miles away from Springer, which means I am halfway through this southbound hike in just nineteen days. Tomorrow I will hike just five miles into Erwin and stay at Uncle Johnny's Hostel, which makes my feet happy. I woke up at 5:00 a.m. this morning and took off hiking at 5:30 a.m. It was pitch black and cloudy, but I liked the early morning silence and the feel of darkness. I hiked slowly at first, but I picked up speed as daylight came. I wanted to get settled in at my destination with daylight to spare, and I arrived at Curley Maple Gap Shelter at 6:30 p.m. The terrain was rough today with an abundance of rocks, roots, uphills, and downhills. Still, it is nowhere near as oppressive as New Hampshire or Maine, so I am counting my blessings. I think that if I book my flight for October 10, I will have plenty of time to make the most of the last of my AT adventure. The AT and I have been through a lot, but we aren't finished yet. Tonight isn't as cold (or as high up) as the last couple of nights, so I don't have to bundle up as much at night. I'm glad I brought cold-weather gear; it has taken care of me. It is only 8:00 p.m., but I am already wrapped up in my sleeping bag, inviting sleep.

September 11

What a happy day. I hiked a quick 5.5 miles into Erwin this morning after a slightly chilly night of good sleep. Just after an hour and a half of leaving the shelter, I found Uncle Johnny's Hostel; I was early enough to make the 9:00 a.m. breakfast shuttle with a thru-hiker named Smiles, who I had read about in trail journals. After breakfast, I showered the spiderwebs from my face, did laundry, and discovered that Yikes was in my neighborhood and looking to meet me to do more hiking. She suggested driving to the hostel and going somewhere for dinner. Who was I to disagree?

I booked my Atlanta to Albuquerque flight for October 9. Having a solid date makes the end feel that much closer. I am eager to get to the Smokies and touch the sky once again. I love the temperatures these days, and I think I'll take my time hiking from now on and stop hiking such big miles. I have no rush, and I want to enjoy my hike. I have about twenty-five days to hike the next 340 miles, so I should make the most of it. Today has been a great chance to let my feet recuperate as I watch a couple of old-school movies; it has been decades since I last saw *The Explorers*. It occurs to me that only after hiking two thousand miles in the last two years can I finally appreciate simple relaxation, the kind where my feet are up, a drink is near, my belly is full, and my plans are going as well as I hoped. I breathe deeply the air of fulfillment, and it nourishes me completely.

September 12

Yikes showed up last night at 7:00 p.m., and we both agreed to a Mexican dinner. We both also agreed that dessert should be Ben & Jerry's Bonnaroo Buzz ice cream accompanied by Yuengling beers, because what are we without our traditions? Up at 6:00 a.m., big breakfast, and hiking at 10:00 a.m. I missed hikes with Yikes; I forgot how fun it was to chat with someone while chewing up the miles. We kept the same pace and discussed our families, hopes, and politics, all while soaking up the effervescence of the trail. She mentioned stopping through Albuquerque on her way to California in early October, and when I told her my travel plans, we decided that she should visit me for a couple of days. I never get tired of hanging out with my friends, and Yikes is one of my favorites. Today, we put down 16 miles, and the temperature dropped considerably when the sun set. It's 323 miles until Springer. I am thinking about hiking smaller days until I get to Hot Springs (52 miles from here), but I'm in love with progress. Yikes doesn't think I'm going to slow down; she's right, it will be difficult to change my pace. I have heard nothing but great things about Elmer's Hostel, even from Yikes; I may keep doing big days just so that I can take a guilt-free zero day there. Having these wonderful options is true happiness.

September 13

I have just 292 miles left to hike! Today's 25 miles led us through wet fields; now I get to put on wet shoes and socks in the morning, hoo-fucking-ray. We passed three northbounders and soaked up the glistening sunlight like sunflowers. Tomorrow, the terrain will be even easier, which makes for a gentle day for happy knees and feet. I think we should hike twenty-one miles tomorrow, making it an easy hike into town the following day. I got a late start this morning at 8:00 a.m.; but that's OK, I plan to get going early tomorrow. At this pace, I will have plenty of time to kill before I fly home; I'll get to explore Atlanta!

It feels like I just left Erwin, but I'm eager to see what Hot Springs is like. Spending time in these amazing little hamlets is one of the understated highlights of doing the AT. Hikers like me must be right up there with poor people and homeless people when it comes to being so grateful for the most everyday conveniences!

September 14

The trail has shown me that no amount of careful planning or logic can weigh in on what actually happens. Case in point: I hiked all twenty-six miles into Hot Springs today with Yikes, and we both decided to rest up at the Laughing Heart Lodge. She planned to hike on to the shelter south of here, but decided a few hours ago that she deserved to stay under a roof tonight. I feel like I earned a zero, so I will get up early and look at staying at Elmer's tomorrow. I have plenty of time, so why the hell not. I suffered long hours and exhausting years at my last job expressly for this hike, so I oughta enjoy my freedom while I have it.

The trail had no roots or mud to negotiate, and the climbs were enjoyably strenuous. Today's hiking began at 7:00 a.m. I paused for an hour-long lunch break at a dilapidated shelter and finished in town with a huge burger and endless refills of root beer at 5:00 p.m. That distance of 271.4 miles never seemed so manageable. I miss things at home that the trail doesn't provide, but I know I will have them soon enough. Tonight I will do my laundry, take a lovely shower, and share the company of this comfortable hostel with my good friend Yikes.

The occasions when Yikes hiked with me were joyous; we both enjoyed the spanning scenery, laughter, deep conversations, and, of course, plenty of frosty cold beverages. The urge for me to sell all my possessions and live a fleeting life between adventures is powerful, and I'm still not sure what keeps me from taking that path instead of the one I find myself on. Could the fear of leaving the familiar be my motivation, or is it the goal of working toward a debt-free life? The sensible part of myself told me it was the latter; I knew it wasn't a bad thing. I had more to choose from than being a materialist, a soul-less automaton, or a minimalist adventurer on a budget, like Jack Kerouac; maybe I could delve into adventuring and *allow myself to have a home and keep a few meaningful possessions. I only hope that I have enough time for all the hikes and excursions that my heart yearns for.*

September 15

Today is my first zero on the trail this year, and I couldn't have picked a better place to take it. I love this place so much that I just might take another zero tomorrow. Yikes and I bade each other a good journey, and then I ate a breakfast of potatoes, eggs, cheese, and diced ham. I also drank a couple of big mugs of that ambrosia I adore.

I ordered new shoes to be sent here when I was in Damascus, so I picked them up at general delivery. They fit so well it was as if Hermes crafted them just for me. I checked in at Elmer's Hostel and couldn't believe my good, no, *great* luck. The mansion is a standing testament to the great hike and all those who dedicated themselves to it. It is stately, gorgeous, and cozy all at once. Elmer is a fine host and an even better cook, if that is possible. This house is full of history and charm and represents a bygone history. I couldn't bear thinking that I would never have experienced it had I not made the decision to hike this trail. Days like today remind me how wonderful a good decision can be, especially when there is so little negativity associated with it. Everyone should feel like this at least once in his or her life, and I fear not enough people do. I put my feet up and treated myself to two of the hostel's movies this afternoon as it rained: *Into the Wild* and *The Way*. Both were appropriate choices that reinforced my hunger for adventure. After I walked around town and had a beer with Stray Dog who had just arrived, I ate two bowls of butternut squash soup, veggie lasagna, and homemade apple pie. The food was so good I had difficulty accepting that it wasn't all a dream. Days like today are fantastic. What will I do when there are no more miles to hike? I shudder at the thought.

September 16

Such a relaxing day surrounded by cozy beauty. Every bite of this morning's breakfast was so important, only last night's dinner could compare to it. The ingredients were fresh, the presentation was above reproach, and the company was stellar. I spent a guilt-free, uneventful zero day filled with beer, *The Darjeeling Limited*, chatting with other hikers, *Empire of the Sun*, and taking in the close proximity of everything.

I didn't just take in the presence of the town; I realized how much excellence there was in my life and how so many important moments have filled the last several months. At the beginning of the summer, I hoped that my Nepal hike would take place without incident and that I could finish this AT hike with just some of the tranquility of spirit and emotional triumph that I felt on Katahdin last year. Now that I am three weeks away from the end, I can't believe my good luck.

Elmer is taking a night off from the kitchen, so I'm going to get dinner at the place across the street that fed me that exquisite breakfast scramble yesterday morning. My plan is to get to Standing Bear Hostel in the next two days, which is at the entrance to Great Smoky National Park, so I don't need to stock up that much on food. The weather has committed to being rainy for the next few days, so I am savoring how dry and clean my feet are today. These days off have boosted my tolerance for the inconveniences ahead. I'm halfway through the book *Idiot America*, and I happen to agree with what the author writes about the "lowest common denominator appeal of American politics." I have enjoyed my time recuperating, but I feel that urge to keep going. I can't let the knowledge that I will be soaked through to my bones deter me from ultimate joy. As long as I have water to drink, what worries do I really have?

September 17

A solid and nutritious breakfast filled me and several other hikers at Elmer's table this morning; we waxed philosophical and political as

I put away the omelet, toast, and tea that were all so good. Honestly, I could have stayed more days at Elmer's, but the desire to continue hiking overcame my love of Hot Springs. I pried myself away and got back on the AT by 11:00 a.m. At 1:00 p.m., rain came down hard and relentlessly. I put over seventeen miles between me and that great little town and am staying at the Roaring Fork Shelter tonight. Three section hikers are staying here, too, and they have very thick New York accents even though they say they're from Florida. The three of us had a pleasant discussion about our very different religious beliefs under a wet, green canopy and fell asleep happy with the miles we all hiked. The double zero in Hot Springs rejuvenated me, and my feet feel bulletproof, no matter how soaked my socks and shoes may be. I almost feel as if I deserve to be rained on for how luxuriously I lived the last couple of days. Tomorrow is just a fourteen-mile hike to the Standing Bear Hostel, which I have heard is worthwhile from other hikers. I think I will cross into Georgia in just two weeks; before I get there I have the stunning Smokies, which fill me with excitement, to traverse. Even though my sleeping bag is a little damp, my spirits are anything but.

September 18

If the AT was any wetter, it would be underwater. The rain persisted all night and didn't let up all day today. I left the shelter at 7:30 this morning, just as my new friends were getting started on their breakfasts. I actually got into the alternating rhythms between the hard and light rainfall. I've been told that reliable forecasts talk of sunshine for the next week, so I hope that every rumored ray of sunlight comes true. I didn't rest until I got to Standing Bear Hostel; once I got there, I immediately decided to stay for the night. The place was filled with friendly souls, and I couldn't tear myself away from the jovial group. I dried my clothes, restocked my food supply to last me through the Smokies, and had some great conversations with the other patrons. I look forward to a dry sleep before I feast my eyes tomorrow upon the best of southern Appalachia. Even now, at dinnertime, it is still raining beyond belief, but I am in a warm bunkroom with food and drinks and feeling healthy. Earlier today I was thoroughly drenched, occasionally chilly, sometimes uncertain I was on the right path, and always eager to be dry after the deluge. I try not to be a princess about these things, but I do love the sensation of dry, warm toes!

September 19

I'm in the Smokies, and I love it. I hiked eighteen miles from Standing Bear to Tricorner Knob Shelter; I climbed almost four thousand feet today. If I hike twenty miles tomorrow, I will then be just two hundred miles away from glorious Springer. I think I will have plenty of time to get to know Atlanta, because I won't take as long to finish the trail as I allowed myself. I am in this shelter with thru-hiker Daniel, the first thru-hiker I met who actually goes by his real name instead of adopting a trail name. There is also a section hiker named Dee here, and ATC ridge runner Billy. These shelters are spacious and roomy enough for plenty, so we are happy tonight. True to the forecast, today's weather was beautifully sunny, and that made for smiles everywhere. I took a break at the Cosby Knob Shelter for almost two hours. The air is cold and crisp, but I'm prepared for it. The Smokies are even more beautiful than what I had hoped.

September 20

What a great day, just the kind that I was looking forward to. It was cold and cloudy when I left the shelter at 7:30 a.m., but the sunshine burned away the mist so that everything was clear by noon, which was exactly when I arrived at Charlies Bunion Loop Trail. I took the short detour, and it was worth it. The vista that greeted me on that side trail was the most rewarding I have seen since I started my hike south in August. I then headed on to take a break at the Icewater Spring Shelter where I ate lunch and had to listen to a seventy-year-old lady's speech about being born again. I had planned to rest there a couple of hours, but the spontaneous religious sermon persuaded me to move on, so I headed off after just forty-five minutes, after she made me promise to read a cartoon pamphlet about Christian salvation. I thought about discussing the possibility of alternate philosophies, but her kind of passion didn't entertain different ideas. I promised that I would read it, so I did, but not with the dedicated seriousness that a Christian soldier would have preferred. I left the pamphlet for someone else to read and spread the good word; maybe they will succeed in faith where I fail. After my truncated break, I was determined to do more miles; maybe I would even get all the way to Clingman's Dome, the highest point on the entire trail.

At almost 6:00 p.m. I enthusiastically arrived at Clingman's Dome. I walked up the looping ramp that offers a panoramic view for miles around. It was sunny and crystal clear; a perfect day to look from Clingman's Dome. I enjoyed the vista, but I didn't have very much time to get to the next shelter before darkness fell. I left Clingman's Dome with an air of satisfaction and arrived at the shelter just before sunset. The shelter was occupied by a group of young day hikers who were loud and obnoxious, but I didn't mind. The group's leader didn't even let me take off my pack before asking me to show him my Great Smoky Mountains National Park permit. I did so curtly and got to making dinner to satisfy an appetite that seemed to have no end.

Later in the evening, the group leader apologized to me for being rude when I arrived; I told him not to worry about it. He didn't seem to believe me when I mentioned how far I hiked today, but he didn't challenge me. I am 140 miles away from Springer now, which seems weirdly impossible. I can't believe tomorrow is my last full day in the Smokies.

The farther south I hiked on the trail, the more I noticed religion taking on a more obnoxious quality that was difficult to avoid and ignore. Since many people hike between semesters and jobs, some religious groups think that the hikers' search for ways to do something amazing with their precious time is really a yearning for answers that only God's true believers can provide. This makes religion a common topic at shelters, and cartoon pamphlets, Bibles, scripture-based comics, and even members of local congregations are always around.

I have been at the receiving end of more than a few looks that range from disapproving to fearful to disgusted once I confessed my happy atheism. As a thirty-six-year-old hiker who wasn't looking for any religious answers, I felt like I was considered persona non grata by everyone who wanted to share the "good news" with the souls that they saw moving through their state.

I usually kept my thoughts to myself and politely listened to Catholics, Baptists, Presbyterians, Southern Baptists, and others impress upon me their singular definitions of right and wrong. I was entertained by how they always tried to appeal to my desire to live a worthwhile life, which was nothing without God and Jesus Christ. I felt like I was being dishonest each time I thanked them before I continued on with my hike because I didn't feel gratitude. The other hikers and I were grateful that we were on a natural high, free from God, substances, and material pleasures. Some of us wondered if we were the ones who should be preaching to the world instead. We never would; we had better things to do.

I endured the looks of disapproval if I happened to be reading a Richard Dawkins book, casually let slip that I didn't think there was a Noah's ark, or didn't agree that the United States was being taken over by the Muslim terrorists or atheist infidels. I suppose I get more wound up by these viewpoints when I'm a city dweller, and I give in to futile attempts to explain myself; in the wilderness and under the trees and stars, I realize that what people believe is between them and their maker.

Ever since Windscreen came alive, I can't be bothered with religious disagreements. The way I see it, we are part of a humongous universe that we know almost nothing about. Whether it all came about because of the wish of a cosmic prime mover or as part of a random confluence of nature over an inconceivable number of eons, this brief glimpse of self-awareness that we have is a mind-blowing concept that I don't want to waste.

September 21

I just can't wrap my head around how quickly these days are passing (symbolic for life, perhaps?) both in time and in distance covered.

Great weather, great pace, great mood. I hiked nineteen miles today to Mollies Ridge Shelter, which claims to be 175 miles from the end of the hike. The Smokies have been absolutely magnificent; I wasn't even bothered by all the day hikers who asked the same questions when they found out I hiked all the way from Roanoke, Virginia. One guy in his forties actually became annoyed with me when I told him how long I've been hiking; he demanded to know what kind of work I was in, how I could take such time off. When I told him I saved money from working as an electrical contractor in Iraq, he reluctantly accepted it before heading off. I'm not sure what he expected, but for some reason he became upset.

In any case, the Smokies have been the best part of this great hike south. Unlike yesterday, I hardly saw anyone as I hiked up Thunderhead after lunch. It wasn't as daunting as the trail journals led me to believe, but it was still pretty challenging. I was the only person hiking along the ridgeline all afternoon; I was afraid that I had accidentally wandered off the AT for most of it, so I was relieved when I saw white blazes painted on the trees again. I met two section hikers at the Russell Field Shelter when I took my dinner break and then continued four more miles before arriving at twilight at Mollies Ridge. I'm alone, which makes for a tranquil and silent evening to admire the stars through the treetops. It's chilly tonight, but I am warm in my clothes, and I will be getting in my sleeping bag soon. I finished *Idiot America* the day before yesterday, and last night I read a small book titled *How to Live on 24 Hours a Day*, which was only OK. I started reading *I'm a Stranger Here Myself* by Bill Bryson; the man consistently delivers the kind of books I love to read. Tomorrow I will descend the mountain into Fontana Dam, just in time for a much-needed resupply.

My feet carried me almost effortlessly through Tennessee, North Carolina, and Georgia. The last two hundred miles were a treat; I had no idea the most southern part of the AT was so easy or beautiful. The way I tackled the AT hike worked out well; getting the hardest part of the trail done first and finishing

*off with the easiest part is actually how I try to arrange my tasks in life. I love
having an easy send-off to whatever I am doing, and the AT reinforced that
mentality. The trail wasn't just getting easier, my entire life was as well. It
was easier emotionally, mentally, and physically. I was streamlined and un-
burdened; there was no guilt, confusion, or occaisional overwhelming loss. I
had recovered from the ravages of Iraq, my brother's death was becoming less
painful, and the academic efforts between the hikes sharpened my mind. I
had never been to self-aware or in total control of everything in my life, and I
liked it at once.*

September 22

Why is the AT not more popular? These days are some of the best
of my entire life. I woke up early and got hiking by 6:30 a.m. The
sun started shining at 7:00 a.m., so I got in a bit of lovely night
hiking. The thrill of the dark gave me an unexpected feeling
of energy and motivation (on top of what was normally there).
The ten miles to Fontana Dam flew, and I rewarded myself for
my quick and relentless pace with four chocolate bars from the
visitors center. I made my way another easy mile and a half and
shuttled into the nearby village for a much-needed resupply at
the general store.

I treated myself to some fried chicken, Gatorade, ice cream, and
coffee while I recharged all my electronic devices. I took a three-hour
break in the touristy, but beautiful town and then headed back out
on the AT by 4:00 p.m. Feeling full and recharged, I made the five-
and-a-half-mile hike to Cable Gap Shelter in good time and decided
on an early bedtime in the hope that I will wake up early for more
night hiking. I will probably get to the Nantahala Outdoor Center, or
NOC, tomorrow since it is just twenty-two miles away. It has been over
a week since I had a proper shower, did laundry, or went online, so
the NOC is a beacon that calls out to my taste for civilization. I have
just 157 miles left on this hike; I am astonished by how effortlessly my
feet have traversed this trail.

September 23

Helluva day. I think I drank too much coffee at the Fontana Dam General Store yesterday; it took me forever to get to sleep last night, instead of dropping off immediately like usual. I lay awake from midnight until 4:00 a.m., when I finally gave up the ghost and decided to get moving. I was sleepy but excited to hike at such an early hour. Unlike some previous early morning departures, this morning was dry and clear; I can't imagine night hiking being much better than it was this morning. There were some treacherous parts, and I took the ups and downs carefully, but the experience was glorious. I never took an official break where I took my pack off my back; I wanted to get to the NOC in time to enjoy most of the day there. I loved watching the sun come up, and the twenty-two miles I hiked today were an absolute dream.

Speaking of dreaming, when I was just six miles away from the NOC, I could see a pretty girl hiking the trail in my direction. The distance closed between us, and I kept thinking to myself how much this hiker looked like Yikes. She even wore her hair the same way and had the same color shorts. I knew it couldn't be her, so I pushed my thoughts away until we got closer. It wasn't until we were five feet apart when I had to believe my eyes. What an unreal surprise it was to see my friend again! It turns out that she has been filling in the places on the AT that she didn't hit last year, and she saved the NOC area for this week when she calculated I would hike through. I couldn't believe it. We exchanged hugs, smiles, and snacks; she accepted one of my Cow Tales candy strips in exchange for one of her delicious pumpkin bagels. After our brief reunion, we continued on our paths since we started shivering seconds after we stopped hiking. We agreed to meet up at the NOC when we were both finished. I am doing laundry now and drinking my fill of water as I warm up on the riverside by the sunshine of the NOC.

I expect Yikes will be here by dinnertime. There is a great-looking restaurant here that will be perfect for us to relax and catch up. I have my eye on the berry crumble, but I can wait for my friend to get back

from her hike while I take this time to respond to phone calls and
e-mails. I found a host today named Brian who agreed to house me
in Atlanta, so I can take comfort knowing that I have a place to stay
for the few days I'll spend there before my flight. I should have made
my departure day sooner, but I couldn't have known there wouldn't
be any unexpected challenges or problems. I can't believe the amazing luck I have had on this trail; seeing Yikes today was something I
would have never even imagined. Life on the AT is better than good;
it's magical.

*I loved the meandering beauty that characterized each day on the AT. It
was on this particularly sunny day that I wrapped up a ninety-mile week of
hiking, which included the splendor of the Smokies, and earned an overnight
at the Nantahala Outdoor Center (or the NOC, if you're a local). I was excited
to get some real food; the siren call of juicy steak, cold craft beer, and how little
I had left to my hike was cause for celebration.*

*Yikes accompanied me for beers and dinner at the NOC, and we settled
comfortably at a table overlooking the Nantahala River. My legs felt like they
were on fire after so many relentless miles up and down mountains, so I didn't
feel at all bad for relaxing where music swam through the air. You wouldn't
think it, but sometimes the best part of hiking is staying still. If you have found
a spot you like, that warms you like a hug, it is worthwhile to sit and relax
there for a spell. Miles can add up to get us farther than we ever thought possible, but the places where we take the time to really drink in what a place has
to offer are where the strongest memories are created.*

*I slept deeply that night at the NOC and woke up the next morning re-
freshed and clean. Yikes and I ate ravenously and decided to soak up the sun,
since it went so very well with our last Ben & Jerry's and beer. I was so close
to the end of my hike, I had to start eating more reasonable amounts and be
health conscious again. It was a sobering realization; the end was nigh.*

September 25

I decided that yesterday would be my last day of hiker excess, so Yikes
and I enjoyed a full day of decadence. I had hiker's breakfast grid-
dles (an impossibly huge serving of scrambled egg-and-vegetables

deliciousness) to start, and then we lazed around by the river and let the sun gently fall on us as we napped. When we woke up, we ate a pint each of, you guessed it, Ben & Jerry's ice cream. For lunch, we devoured between us what the restaurant called a "lotza protein" pizza, followed by peach crumble with vanilla ice cream for dessert. Feeling like we were neglecting a food group, I ordered a bottle of merlot. After all that, it was time to hit the trail. Rather than hike north to where she left her car, Yikes headed south with me to Wesser Tower. It was just a six-mile jaunt, which was good since we were nicely buzzed. We both packed out a small box of pinot noir each; we drank one at the three-mile marker and the other atop Wesser Tower, where we stopped for the night.

There is nothing that makes my heart sing more than unblemished nature, especially when it is bathed in the light of a sunset. It got chilly, but the sleeping bags were warm enough, even with the wind whipping around the tent at the top of the tower. We woke up a tad hungover, but in time to see the inspirational sunrise. For breakfast, we ate pumpkin-flavored Clif Bars and Cow Tales. After an hour of relaxing under the early morning sky, I hugged Yikes, told her to call me whenever she was in Albuquerque, and got back on the AT. With just over a week left to the hike, I didn't expect to see anyone else I knew on the trail, even Yikes; but then again, the AT defies all expectations.

After the 15 miles I hiked today, I have just 113 more to go. The terrain was excellent and so was the weather. I crossed paths with a couple of hikers today who highly recommended a hostel that would be well worth my time, so I decided to check it out. I am not disappointed in the slightest. The hostel is actually a great cabin, the kind that people spend hundreds to stay at; it has all the amenities of a hotel. I got cleaned up and took up the host's offer for both dinner and breakfast. The prices are reduced for thru-hikers, who only have to pay fifteen dollars per night instead of the usual price for vacationers, who pay a hundred dollars more. I have the place to myself, and I am finally rehydrated after partying at the NOC. I am fully nourished by the roast chicken, mashed potatoes, and vegetables and have enjoyed taking a load off my feet and getting some reading done.

This coming week looks to be a relatively gentle end to a beautiful adventure, so I am working on eating less so that my body won't keep craving calories when I get back to academic life. The trail has affected me in more ways than I am probably aware of, but I have noticed I appreciate the beauty that will just be if we let things grow. I have also learned how important it is to make the most of the time that I have in this short life. The thing is, I thought I knew all about these things before I even set foot on the AT, but I barely scratched the surface. Good times, good friends, good fortune, and good hiking promises to complete what was two years ago a crazy ambition. There are things that I know so much about, and then there are things that I know absolutely nothing about; I am fascinated by both and want more.

Wesser Tower gave us an untrammeled vantage point for seeing as far the eye possibly could, so we didn't miss the natural concert around us. It stands out as one of my favorite places on the trail. We watched as the sun poked up above the tree line in the distance before we rolled up the tent and packed up our bags. We ate our last trail breakfast together, agreed to meet again in Albuquerque, and took off in opposite directions. I had a good chunk of the trail left to finish, but the worst was behind me. Unlike the Hundred-Mile Wilderness of the north terminus, this section was more like a hundred-mile cooldown.

I was blindsided by a reluctance to rejoin a society that depended too heavily on material wealth and objects for fulfillment. If I wasn't mostly certain that I wanted to keep owning a house, I would have immediately sold it so I wouldn't have to be bothered with whoring my résumé out to a thousand recruiters and employers with the sole intent to make enough money to pay off my mortgage. I wasn't certain what job I would take next. I only knew that it would be overseas, and I would try to find one that was as meaningful as possible. Maybe in a couple of years I would save enough to hike the PCT.

September 26

Today was as perfect a hiking day as I could get. I woke up well rested in the cozy cabin at 7:30 a.m. and watched *Tropic Thunder* as I packed.

At 8:00 a.m. the hostess brought breakfast, and I was beside myself. The local coffee was delicious, the waffles were plentiful, and the blueberries were fresh from her garden. It was a great start to the day, and I felt powerful enough to hike the rest of the trail without stopping. Instead, I hiked just fifteen miles and am tenting at the Big Spring Shelter. The original plan was to do longer miles (and I certainly feel up to doing them), but I am planning to meet Michaela who wants to hike the Georgia portion of the trail with me; it is in my best interest to do fewer miles so she can meet me when she gets her days off. It is an odd feeling to conform to someone else's parameters. I'm preparing to live off the trail now, and nothing represents that more than having to work with other people and share time. I have only eighty-two miles and seven days until she meets up with me at Suches, Georgia. If I had even the slightest amount of stress when it came to pacing myself (which I didn't), I certainly don't now. In fact, it just occurred to me that I have hiked my last twenty-mile day on the AT. This makes me feel a bit sad. On the other hand, I'm still excited to see my friend and then make my way to Atlanta, so I am upbeat. I have 98.6 miles to go until I summit Springer Mountain.

September 27

Change of plans (aren't there always changes to the best-laid plans?). Today was my final twenty-plus-mile day, since I was motivated to hike all the way to the Plum Orchard Shelter. I hiked twenty-seven miles, and I feel great. I am now just seventy-two miles away from Springer Mountain. I feel like I could almost see it if I just squint hard enough. It was a great relief to come across this beautiful shelter, not to mention the flowing stream nearby that I so desperately needed.

I plan to hike just fifteen miles tomorrow to a shelter near Unicoi Gap. I passed the famous gnarly tree this afternoon; it was beautiful to finally see after hearing about it so many times. I suppose it wouldn't be a big deal anywhere else, but on the AT, that tree might as well be a sign for southbound hikers saying, "Come on, you're nearly finished!" Just past the gnarly tree was the state line between North

Carolina and Georgia. I stood with each foot in a different state, not knowing when I would get to straddle states again. I reflected on a great many things on that state line, like how much could have gone wrong, or how many times I could have hurt myself during this hike. None of my worst fears came to pass. Tonight, I will choose a new book from my Kindle since I finished my Bill Bryson book today. New state, new book. Tomorrow will feel different since everything is getting so much easier, but the change of pace is good preparation for the greater changes that are waiting for me off the trail at home. My thoughts linger on John Manifold's wedding, my final semester, and job hunting in the new year. The next seventy-two miles don't stand a chance.

September 28
More changing of plans: Why am I not surprised? I made today a short one and hiked into Hiawassee to stock up on food and get a warm meal. I had stopped cooking meals a few days ago, opting to not burden myself with the added weight of denatured alcohol for the final days of the hike. Instead, I have been subsisting on Clif Bars, trail mix, and dried fruit. The Chinese buffet in town was just what I needed; I remembered to not overeat, but I wanted to. I chatted with John to let him know I was almost done hiking, and we locked in the dates that I would be in Phoenix. I am excited to see my friend and attend his wedding. I had my last pint of Ben & Jerry's ice cream tonight, and I must confess that I never get tired of sleeping in a proper bed. The motel is cheap and near to everything, so I am comfortably happy. I plan to hike twenty miles tomorrow and the day after, and I arranged earlier today to be shuttled from the AT to the hostel where Michaela would meet me on Monday. Just sixty-seven miles to go.

September 29
I hiked nineteen miles today to the Blue Mountain Shelter. An AT dweller named Randy and a Belgian hiker who doesn't know much English are staying here tonight as well. Randy is the third AT dweller

I've met. The other two I met were on my northbound hike last year. These guys intrigue me; they bounce between shelters each day to avoid being around the same hikers so it isn't obvious that they are homeless. They have my sympathy, but I wonder how they expect so many keen-eyed hikers to believe their stories about how they have been hiking for hundreds of miles when they are wearing jeans and carrying heavy-duty propane stoves that would offend any thru-hiker. The dwellers I met just want to be left alone, so I only speak as much as courtesy demands. I don't bother them with my stories, and they don't ask me much. I know that if I asked Randy when he started hiking and why he started so late, he would have a prepared answer. If I point out that his jeans are a better choice for homeless living instead of high-performance hiking, he might have a snappy or humorous response. I have no wish to shame my neighbor, so I admit my tiredness and read the shelter logbook. I hope that Randy and the other vagabonds find success and peace in their lives.

There was rain first thing this morning, but the sun shone from noon through the end of the day. By the time I got to the shelter, my clothes were damp, mostly from sweat. I am a little less than 50 miles from Springer (48.7 to be exact), and I am so silently happy. There is something wonderful about being on the threshold of accomplishment, and I am barely able to contain my excitement. Tomorrow looks to be an easy day, but I would love it even if it was a day filled with Pennsylvania rocks, Vermont mosquitoes, Maine black flies, New Hampshire ups and downs, and Tennessee religious cartoon pamphlets stapled to every tree. I am on cloud nine, and nothing can get me down.

September 30
Blood Mountain tonight. The stone cabin shelter on the mountaintop was built in the 1950s, and it looks like I'll be the only resident in it tonight. I wish that the cabin had a door to keep out the wind and mist, but I must admit that having four mostly solid walls is damn near a luxury out here. I am twenty-eight miles from Springer

now. Tomorrow I have an eight-mile hike to the trailhead at Woody Gap, where my hosts will pick me up at noon. That means I don't need to leave the shelter until 8:00 a.m., so I can wake up relatively late. This morning, I woke up early and started night hiking at 6:15 a.m. I arrived at Neels Gap by 1:30 p.m. and relaxed at the friendly store for a couple of hours. The weather is perfect for Halloween, and there were dozens of pumpkins and brightly colored autumn leaves. I read my book, ate a couple of microwaved meals, and had plenty of water and Gatorade. Although I was the only thru-hiker I saw all day, I was glad to feel a part of the hiking community and spirit at Neels Gap. I made the climb up Blood Mountain and was surprised by the near effortlessness of it. I felt damn near superhuman. Once I got to the peak, I looked around, found the beautiful stone shelter, and made a place to sleep for myself before I prepared my dinner. There was a young couple named Tim and Samantha at the top burning sandalwood incense; the aroma reminded me instantly of New Mexico. We chatted awhile; they could tell how happy I was being on the threshold of victory. They headed down before sunset, and I watched the heavy clouds roll in slowly to insulate me from the gorgeous scenery. The constant drizzle made the stone shelter a comfortable place to read and write by headlamp in the comfort of my sleeping bag. Earlier I shared half of my water (about a liter) with a couple of hikers who were desperate for it. They were immeasurably grateful, and I wondered if I reacted with the same wild gratitude when I was met with such kind generosity all those times during the long hike.

I can never forget how this trail brings out the best in people. I don't want to stop staring at the palate of color all around me, even though I can barely see any of it anymore. The waning light only shows more of the forest's ever-changing beauty instead of less.

This place fills me with the spookiness of the season in the way I always want around this time of year. It isn't difficult to imagine werewolves, vampires, and foul creatures inhabiting these woods, and I feel exuberance instead of fear.

October 2

Yesterday was my first rainy hike since the day I hiked to the Standing Bear Hostel. I woke up at about 5:30 a.m. to pouring rain that fell loudly on the soaked ground and trees outside. Although I was drenched by the morning hike, the eight miles passed quickly. I deliberately took my time so I wouldn't have to wait long at the trailhead. Even at a slow pace, the hike lasted only three hours; I actually enjoyed being thoroughly soaked because I knew I would be warm and dry by lunchtime. Right on time, the driver came and spirited me to the hostel, which was a sight for sore eyes.

This hostel is the last in a long line of charming places I have stayed along the trail and leaves me wanting for nothing. The place is clean and inviting, and this time of year it isn't crowded like it must be at peak season. I read and watched a few movies as I waited patiently for Michaela to arrive.

A father-daughter hiking pair took me to dinner with them in exchange for answering any and all their questions about the trail, which I agreed to with enthusiasm. The following morning, I woke up to the most amazing smell from the kitchen upstairs. The group breakfast was as hearty as it was delicious, and I took care not to overeat since I had so few miles to go. I am clean, dry, and ready to finally put the AT on my list of accomplishments.

October 2

Today was a crazy day; some good, some bad. My stuff was packed and I was ready to go, so I read for an hour in the upstairs loft until Michaela arrived. Just as I finished Joseph Conrad's *Heart of Darkness*, I heard her car pull up. I thanked my hosts, and we left immediately to hike in the gorgeous sunshine. Michaela assured me that she had been getting in shape for the next couple of days of hiking, but I still had a feeling that she had underestimated the AT. We started heading south on the trail at 1:00 p.m., with the plan to hike 12.5 miles. After the first few miles of hiking with her, I could see that she had severely underestimated the AT. I slowed my pace and paused for her to catch up several times an hour. I was amazed by the huge pack she carried; I wondered what she had packed for just two days. I suppose the army doesn't teach soldiers to pack light.

After five miles, we took a break at the Gooch Mountain Shelter and had a snack. Hiking the next seven miles took it out of her, and she moved along at an infuriatingly slow pace. I could see that she was upset with how difficult she found the trail and was discouraged at every incline. I offered to take some of her supplies into my pack to lighten her load, but she was a trooper and insisted on carrying everything she packed out. I admired her tenacity, even if it was accompanied by moans and complaints. Before long, her feet were giving her trouble, and I became worried that we wouldn't make it to our destination before twilight. I knew that hiking in the dark would only add to her frustrations, so I encouraged her to see through the pain and fight on. The closer we got to the shelter, she slower she moved; then she began feeling light-headed. I urged her to rest and drink water, but I think the exhaustion was more than she was prepared for.

We slowly made progress until I saw the beautiful signpost that pointed us toward the shelter that was hidden behind some trees. I have never seen anyone so happy to arrive at a shelter, and that is saying something, considering all the scares, bad weather, and treacherous climbs that I have experienced. She got settled in her sleeping bag as I replenished our water supplies. She pulled out some granola bars and trail mix for dinner. I think she prayed for the strength to hike the remaining eight miles to Springer Mountain and her car. The selfish part of me is glad that she didn't make it out here sooner, or we definitely wouldn't be as close to the end as we are now; she would have hated Blood Mountain. I was still happy to see my friend, even though she was in too much pain to care much about the joys of hiking. Tonight is my last overnight on the AT, and I can scarcely believe it.

October 3

I have completed the Appalachian Trail!

Last night I slept well, despite being as excited as a kid on Christmas Eve; it was the same as the night before I summited Katahdin last year. Michaela fell asleep early while I read *Darkly Dreaming Dexter*. The shelter was filled with day and section hikers. Everyone stirred awake at 8:00 a.m. and began making breakfast jovially and playing music. I let Michaela enjoy the Appalachian morning at her leisure; I would miss the tranquility of these mornings on the trail. She was a bit more reluctant than I was, but she put on a brave face, and we were ready to hike by 9:00 a.m. I thought Michaela might have an easier time today, but it wasn't long before she started complaining; her feet and legs just weren't used to more than five miles while carrying so much weight. It reminded me of my own foot problems when I was getting used to the hike last year, so I sympathized. We continued to close the distance between us and the goal, and I was grateful that there wasn't any difficult terrain. In fact, I was amazed at how so clean, level, and smooth to hike the trail was. The weather was sunny with gentle breezes, so I was personally enjoying the day as much as Michaela was suffering it.

After 6.5 miles, we arrived at Michaela's car. She was ready to stop hiking, but she arranged to meet me on the other side of Springer Mountain at the Amicalola Falls Visitor Center. After making sure that she was OK, I put on my pack one last time and attacked Springer Mountain. I was wearing my Superman socks from Sensei, and they flew me up that mountain with ease. On the top, I found the famous plaque that marks the southern terminus of the AT; since there wasn't a single soul on the mountain besides me, so I was permitted to reflect in solitude.

I faced north and took time to remember all of the days, people, and significant events and moments that took place on this incredible journey, and I accepted that the last day was here. The end of the journey is now. I read the entire journal that is kept in a drawer under the plaque, safe from the elements, and contributed my thoughts. I couldn't decide what I felt more this afternoon: pleasure or sadness. The place itself was really more of a blink-and-you-miss-it area. If the small monument hadn't been there, I wouldn't have been sure that this was the all-important southern terminus. The prize reflected the hike itself, less flash, but more substance. The hike, which began after years of hoping and months of planning, was over. Tomorrow I would be a normal person again.

I was lost in thought when an older couple joined me at the mountaintop. They were breathing heavily, but thrilled to be there as well. They told me they started at the parking lot where Michaela's hike ended. I told them, as modestly as I could, where I started. They bombarded me with questions, and I happily answered. I asked them to take my picture at the top to commemorate the end of the hike, and they were honored.

After an hour of being on Springer, I decided to take time to figure my emotions and thoughts out during the eight-and-a-half-mile hike to Amicalola Falls. I thanked the kind couple for their time and began the extra hike to Amicalola Falls. I remember Face telling me how unnecessary this part of the hike was, but I was glad to do it anyway.

The final stretch was a serene opportunity for me to come to terms with what completion meant and to look to the future with the same optimism and excitement that I faced each morning on the AT. I arrived in good spirits at the visitors center at 5:00 p.m. and found Michaela sound asleep in her car. She smiled when I woke her up and started the car with gusto as I loaded my pack in the trunk. We were both in the mood for steak and beer, so I began to search through the list of restaurants in her GPS as she pulled away from the AT, neither of us looking back.

EPILOGUE

When I ascended Springer Mountain on October 2, 2012, I couldn't have been in better spirits. I stood at the AT plaque and attempted to grasp the reality of being there. My AT experience had begun a year and a half earlier and had brought more experiences into my life than I could fully comprehend. The towns, the personalities, the natural gorgeousness, and the progress of every mile helped me to form a better idea of what I wanted to do in this life. I wasn't looking for answers or reinvention, but the AT still changed my life. I liked being Windscreen and wanted to become him again, even if it wouldn't be for another few years.

From the start I met some incredible characters on the trail. Everyone was happy to set a few months aside to get away from their normal lives or go on an adventure between jobs or semesters. It was refreshing to meet a different sort of culture than what I had spent most of my life around. The culture I embraced in the air force was proud but in many ways was entitled and single-minded. Many amazing people hiked the trail alongside me, whether it was for just a day, a week, a month, or through until the finish, and I was glad to see what everyone was about. I am happy to say I am still in touch with many of them; whenever we meet up or chat on the phone, it is always energetic and heartfelt.

On the last day of my hike, I contacted Stillwater (of the Fellowship) who I hadn't seen since we partied in Monson the previous year. I knew that he was attending college near Amicalola Falls, and I wanted to get together while I was in his neighborhood. The next day he picked me up at my hotel and I said good-bye to Michaela before she returned to Fort Benning. Stillwater and his girlfriend were heading to Atlanta the next day, so he happily agreed to give me a ride to my couch-surfing host. We compared our experiences on the AT, chatted about our lives off the trail, and didn't let a silent minute pass between us for the entirety of those two days. Like so many other AT alums, we remain in touch still.

My couch-surfing experience in Atlanta surpassed all of my expectations. My host Brian and his roommate Louis were friendly, hospitable, and eager to hear everything I could tell them about the AT. They had a comfortable couch for me to sleep on, and their house was situated conveniently within walking distance of downtown Atlanta. It makes me chuckle to use the term "walking distance" after completing the AT, but there we are. I went skydiving with Brian, and we ate good meals together and toured the local area in his free time. Staying in their house for those few days gave me the opportunity to upload and share my pictures online, chat with friends and family to let them know where (and how) I was, and adjust to life off the trail again. Brian and Louis graduated shortly after that; Brian got a job in San Diego as an accountant, and Louis visited Albuquerque on his journey west to hike the PCT. I followed Louis's comments and pictures with great interest, and we still chat extensively about the trails under our belts whenever we are both online.

It was my pleasure and honor to be John's best man. John, his groomsmen, and I rented matching tuxedos that made us look sharp, and I didn't look like Windscreen at all. In under two weeks I became a well-dressed, clean-cut, sweet-smelling functional member of society again; I even traded my Merrill Moabs for spitshined slip-on shoes. I wasn't disappointed, but I certainly didn't want to lose touch with the guy who hiked all thoe miles. I owed Windscreen a lot; he did all the emotional and spiritual heavy lifting that I never got around to doing. John's wedding was spectacular, with endless food-stuffs, beverages, dances, and songs to sing along with badly. The wedding was the picture of civilized frivolity.

I saw Yikes in Albuquerque as we arranged, and she stayed for a week to recover from the ultramarathon she ran just days prior. Pants also visited during that time and went with me and Yikes to Albuquerque's Balloon Fiesta. Sensei stopped through Albuquerque and stayed in my home for a couple nights on his way from Texas to

Colorado, and we waxed enthusiastic about our AT adventure. It is always an honor to share my home with friends, especially these folks, who slept in tents and shelters with me up and down the AT. Other reunions included meeting up with Johnny Appleseed in Brooklyn when I visited Occupy Wall Street and meeting up with Spam, Sensei, and Pants in Denver for indoor climbing, drinks, and laughs. I barely missed seeing Leaf Guy when he came to work in New Mexico after I went to work in Saudi Arabia. I still chat with several others I hiked with on the trail and I hope to cross paths with them again in the future.

I'm inundated by memories from that other world. I can feel the cool breeze, the warm sunshine, and the worn-out shoes that sheathed bulletproof feet. I recall depositing my brother's ashes as clearly right now as if I were still there, and I'll never forget the euphoria of drinking water after half a day of hiking without it. The weight bearing on my back and legs hurt at first, but the pain was nothing compared to the beauty of everything. Even now, my brain is still trying to absorb everything that happened during those incredible months. No matter how easy and sheltered life is when I'm at home or working at a job, I never stop thinking about trail life, especially here in this sandy world of brown and beige. Nobody I have met in this country, Saudi or American, has ever attempted a thru-hike, and I'm not sure any of my compatriots here want to. Windscreen doesn't belong here, but he looks forward to next summer when he will fly again.

I can't ignore the calling of the trail; the more I read about and look at pictures of the Pacific Crest Trail, the more it becomes an obsession. I also want to hike the Camino de Santiago in Europe, New Zealand's Te Araroa, and maybe the Continental Divide Trail as well, but I have to be patient while I earn money. Fortunately, I have a job that cultivates my skills and fulfills me, but I am looking forward to the future when I will go by Windscreen again. I hunger for that wild adventure that only hiking the trail can provide, so I am counting down the months until I start on the PCT. That hike will be different from the AT in that I intend to hike the entirety of it instead of breaking it into two sections. There will also be fewer town visits, the mileage per day will be greater, the elevation changes won't be as drastic, and water will be scarcer. Most importantly, I'll have the unbridled support of my entire family, with none of the guilt. My brother and mother are proud of what I have achieved, and it pleases them to tell my adventures to their friends and neighbors. I look forward to discovering the trail's character and exploring three of the most beautiful states in the country. The PCT hike will be a welcome break after working as a technical instructor in Saudi Arabia for two years, and I am grateful for the opportunity to make it a reality. At the time of this writing, I have just over half a year to save money and plan the details of this next hike, and each day brings greater anticipation and excitement.

I hesitate to guess what next year's adventure will be like, but I know it will be infinitely rewarding.

Here's to the journey!

Made in the USA
Lexington, KY
19 December 2014